D0985819

APPLIED
interpretation

Putting Research into Practice

i n t e r p P r e s s

NATIONAL ASSOCIATION FOR
INTERPRETATION

P.O. Box 2246
Fort Collins, CO 80522

NAI is a private nonprofit [501(c)3] organization and
professional association. NAI's mission is: "Inspiring
leadership and excellence to advance heritage
interpretation as a profession." For information, visit
www.interpnet.com.

ISBN 978-1-879931-23-0

On the cover: Interpretive program at Great Smoky
Mountains National Park / author photo

Dedicated to the Loves of My Life

Julie, Madeline, and Jacob

.

CONTENTS

ACKNOWLEDGMENTS

This book is the product of 16 years of research that was conducted at a variety of federal, state, and local parks and resource sites. Therefore, there are numerous agencies and individuals whose support and work were crucial to this book. In particular, the Department of Recreation, Park, and Tourism Studies at Indiana University, the National Park Service, the United States Forest Service, the National Park Foundation, and the National Environmental Education and Training Foundation offered financial and institutional support.

There are also many individuals who aided in the design, collection, and analysis of the research studies used for this book. Dr. Gregory Benton, in particular, was an invaluable colleague for many of the studies and subsequent publications. Mr. James Farmer has also been an important influence in the research and the development of this book. Others include Dr. Elizabeth Barrie, Dr. Raymond Poff, Dr. James Sibthorp, Dr. Harold Hungerford, Dr. Trudi Volk, Ms. Tracy Drake, Mr. Sean Marsan, Ms. Gretchen Monimee-Faherty, Ms. Karen Bareford, and Ms. Jessica Aycock.

FOREWORD

by Sam H. Ham

When I was a student 35 years ago, one of my cognitive psychology professors assigned a reading that he claimed would "turn memory research on its ear." The author of the article, a Canadian psychologist named Endel Tulving, seemed to do just that. Tulving's research had demonstrated that a lot of standard memory tests weren't actually measuring people's memory of factual information. Instead, what they measured was memory of the experience of being exposed to that information. In other words, what these people were actually remembering was an event in which they had been a participant. Tulving called this "episodic memory" (or "autobiographical memory"), which psychologists today 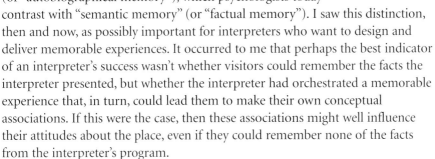 contrast with "semantic memory" (or "factual memory"). I saw this distinction, then and now, as possibly important for interpreters who want to design and deliver memorable experiences. It occurred to me that perhaps the best indicator of an interpreter's success wasn't whether visitors could remember the facts the interpreter presented, but whether the interpreter had orchestrated a memorable experience that, in turn, could lead them to make their own conceptual associations. If this were the case, then these associations might well influence their attitudes about the place, even if they could remember none of the facts from the interpreter's program.

Since then, I have continued to follow episodic memory research hoping to see someone in the interpretation field latch onto the notion. This happened in the late 1990s when a professor at Indiana University, Doug Knapp, began publishing articles on the role of episodic memory in interpretation and environmental education. He began looking at the memories adults and children actually took away from interpretive encounters and noticed that, while their recall of factual information was usually quite poor, their ability to recall other aspects of the experience was much stronger. Linking these findings to Tulving's episodic memory model, his growing body of research has been able to bring interpreters a fresh new perspective on the possible impacts of their programs. If visitors could vividly recall their experiences in a place, might those same recollections serve as anchors for making conceptual associations imparted by interpretation? *Applied Interpretation: Putting Research into Practice* offers answers to this question in a way that no other volume before has attempted. It is the result of a significant body of research that stands to guide our thinking about the interpretation process for years to come.

In eight very readable chapters, this book presents a rationale for looking at interpretation through the eyes of episodic memory in an impressive range of applications. These include programs for large and small groups, programs in parks and nature centers, and programs aimed at adults as well as schoolchildren. In each chapter, Knapp draws the reader into his thinking and presents relevant research findings in support of the conclusions he draws. In all my years in the interpretation business, I have found no other volume that has brought together such a depth of one person's research in such a thoughtful way. It is in some respects a sort of "opus in progress."

Readers who turn these pages will be treated to a fresh and careful analysis of the outcomes interpretive programs are actually capable of producing. The result of this analysis is encouraging because it provides an evidence-based framework within which every interpreter can achieve success. That is, even when visitors can remember little of what an interpreter showed or said to them, the interpreter's impact can be seen in their recollection of what happened on the day and how they felt about it. Knapp's research suggests that active engagement in the interpretation process produces stronger episodic memory in visitors and that intertwined with these recollections are visitors' own conceptual understandings of what makes the place special or important to them. In 1957, Freeman Tilden referred to these associations as "personal truths." He argued that the interpreter's job is not to teach anyone anything in the didactic sense, but rather to provoke them to do their own thinking and to make their own meanings. Studies conducted in just the past 10 years back up Tilden's advice, and by extension, Knapp's thesis. They show that the more a communicator succeeds in provoking an audience to think, the less likely those people are to do well on a test of the facts that were actually presented. This conclusion is at the heart of Knapp's research. Indeed, it is not very surprising that days or months following an interpretive program, he finds that visitors are able to talk at length about what the experience meant to them, even though little of what they have to say is identical to the actual content presented.

Three decades after Tulving's breakthrough, research on episodic memory has consistently shown us that simply maintaining factual information in short-term memory (which is what most evaluations of interpretive programs continue to measure) is a poor indicator of long-term learning. When we evaluate an interpretive encounter based on how many of the interpreter's facts a visitor can remember, we cannot assume or demonstrate that superior recall will have anything to do with how that visitor will think or feel or behave tomorrow. The number of studies in support of this conclusion is staggering, and they have been conducted not only in psychology laboratories, but in free-choice learning environments such as parks, museums, zoos, aquaria, visitor centers, and other interpretive settings. However, despite the weight of accumulated evidence, we have continued to evaluate interpretive programs as didactic encounters in which visitor-students are expected to remember the interpreter's content. It is my hope that *Applied Interpretation: Putting Research into Practice* will serve as a turning point in our understanding of the interpretation process and that it stimulates interpreters everywhere to see themselves as provokers of profound personal meaning, rather than as bearers of entertaining facts. When visitors make meanings, they make memories. And memories are a worthy outcome of any interpretive encounter.

Sam H. Ham, Ph.D.
Professor
Department of Conservation Social Sciences
University of Idaho

1. Applying Research to Interpretation

Introduction

Every year, millions of people visit national, regional, and local parks. Many of these people will seek some type of information about or understanding of the sites they visit. This information may come in the form of a brief stop along a highway to view a panorama, a walk along the shoreline of a lake, a tour of a nature center, or an evening program at a campground. Thousands of park and recreation personnel are engaged in processes that provide visitors with high-impact, short-term experiences. The process of "revealing" natural, cultural, and historical wonders is what Freeman Tilden called *interpretation* in 1957.

A variety of outcomes are desired from participation in these interpretive programs—from art appreciation to understanding zoological phenomena. Along with the range of programs comes a variety of resources for interpreters to use to help achieve these outcomes. These works include Freeman Tilden's *Interpreting Our Heritage*, Sam Ham's *Environmental Interpretation: A Practical Guide for People with Big Ideas and Small Budgets*, and Doug Knudson's *Interpretation of Cultural and Natural Resources*. Although they are excellent resources, these and many other books and training guides are based on beliefs, premonitions, and literature related to other fields. In fact, even today, the field of interpretation continues to use Freeman Tilden's book as a basis for the profession of interpretation—a work written by *one man 50 years ago.*

Research Approach

This work is an attempt to offer the field of interpretation strategies, methods, experiences and other programmatic variables that have been found through research to have lasting impacts on visitors. The case studies, scenarios, and findings found in the forthcoming chapters are a product of 15 years of research in the field of interpretation, environmental education, and science education. Therefore, the content is set apart from other resources due to its reliance on research—and not conjecture.

The methods taken to analyze the range of interpretive experiences outlined in the following chapters follow two general tracks—quantitative and qualitative analysis. The primary distinction between the two is that qualitative data involves words and quantitative data involves numbers. Another difference between the two is that qualitative research is inductive and quantitative research is deductive. In inductive, qualitative research, a hypothesis is not needed to begin research. On the other hand, deductive, quantitative research requires a hypothesis before research can begin. Another difference between qualitative and quantitative research is the underlying assumptions about the role of the researcher. In qualitative research, it is thought that the researcher can learn the most about a situation by participating in and/or being immersed in it. In quantitative research, however, the researcher is, ideally, an objective observer that neither participates in nor influences what is being studied.

Since the objective of this book is to offer findings that can be applied to the interpreter in the field, the research methods associated with the findings are described in general layman terms. Further information regarding the "nuts and bolts" of the analysis, methodologies, instrument development and results can be found in abstracts of each research study found in the appendix of this book.

Each approach has its drawbacks. Qualitative research sometimes focuses too closely on individual results and fails to make connections to larger situations or possible causes of the results. Quantitative research, on the other hand, often "forces" responses or people into categories that might not "fit" in order to make meaning. Despite their limitations, they are important avenues to use to learn how interpretation impacts the visitor.

Quantitative Studies

The quantitative methods used for this book represent surveys and questionnaires given to visitors prior to and following interpretive programs. In some cases, participants were given surveys and questionnaires immediately after the experience and/or three to 18 months after their interpretive program or school

Sample One

1. Please complete this sentence: The thing I remember most about my trip to Thomson Park was: _____.

2. List three activities you did during the program at Thomson Park.

3. What activity did your program leader do to help you learn how a tree transpires?

4. Choose the sentence that best describes how you feel:
   _____a. I would like to go to Thomson Park and spend more time learning about plants.
   _____b. I would rather go to another park to learn more about plants.
   _____c. I would not like to go to a park to learn more about plants.

Sample Two

Read each statement carefully and circle the rating that best represents your opinion:

1. If I were a spelunker (caver), it would not bother me to have to get a key to unlock a gate to get into local caves.

   Strongly agree   Agree   Undecided   Disagree   Strongly disagree

2. Timbering practices must be stopped in order to protect the Indiana bat.

   Strongly agree   Agree   Undecided   Disagree   Strongly disagree

3. Extinction is a natural process. Using tax dollars to save endangered species like the Indiana bat is wasteful.

   Strongly agree   Agree   Undecided   Disagree   Strongly disagree

4. Given the opportunity, I would assist in bat conservation efforts.

   Strongly agree   Agree   Undecided   Disagree   Strongly disagree

5. There is no significant role that bats play that entitles them to protection.

   Strongly agree   Agree   Undecided   Disagree   Strongly disagree

field trip. Samples from two evaluation instruments can be found on page 3. The first is a questionnaire given to students 18 months following an interpretive field trip to a city park. The second sample includes questions that were given to visitors prior to and immediately after a campfire program.

The responses from these surveys and questionnaires were then analyzed using a variety of statistical methods. Below is an excerpt from a published research article on the impacts of two different types of interpretive field trips at Indiana Dunes National Lakeshore. This edited piece overviews the methodology of this study and is indicative of the type of quantitative analysis used by the author:

Methods and Procedures

This study evaluated the impact of two different interpretive experiences on elementary students' knowledge, attitude, and/or behavior toward the resource site they were visiting. Subjects were taken from fourth, fifth and sixth grades in three urban school districts in northern Indiana. The participants represented a diverse cultural and ethnic background with a predominant percentage being black and Hispanic. Approximately 1,500 students participated in both programs, representing 705 fourth graders, 637 fifth graders and 213 sixth graders. These students were taken to the Indiana Dunes National Lakeshore for a half-day interpretive program once in the fall of 1995 and once in the spring of 1996. Both field trips were designed to be conducted in an outdoor setting and experiential in method. The only difference between the two field trips was the content of the interpretive program. The fall session covered basic ecological concepts while the spring concentrated on environmental issues relative to the park.

To evaluate the impact the programs had on students' knowledge, attitudes, and behavior toward the environment, a quasi-experimental design (Isaac & Michael, 1990) was implemented using an evaluation instrument that included 15 multiple-choice questions. This was a replication of an evaluation tool developed by Drake and Knapp (1994) and Bluhm, Hungerford, McBeth, and Volk (1995). The validity of this evaluation was established by a critique jury made up of Indiana Dunes interpreters, who observed that the instrument did reflect information, attitudes, and behaviors desired following a park program.

A Repeated Measures MANOVA (multivariate analysis of variance) was used to evaluate all 15 multiple-choice questions. This analysis was chosen to determine if the difference in responses over time was significant. Each question on the evaluation instrument was examined to determine if a significant change occurred in students' knowledge, attitudes, and/or behavior intent as a result of attending either interpretive experience. Two control classes representing approximately 70 students were evaluated and compared with the results of the experimental population during the fall session. Three control groups representing approximately 85 students were used in the spring (Knapp & Barrie, 2001).

Results of these quantitative approaches were then published in several research journals and field periodicals in interpretation and science education.

Qualitative Studies
Qualitative analysis has been the most successful strategy to learn the impacts of an interpretive experience. There are several reasons for its advantage over quantitative approaches. First, the researcher has the ability to interview visitors to probe for their own feelings or impacts related to a program. This type of inquiry offers much more insight than pencil-and-paper surveys. Another important advantage of the interview approach is its ability to "hone in" on the actual interpretive experience—especially months or years following a program. For instance, when sixth graders were interviewed *three years* after a program at a nature center, the researcher(s) had a complete list of what was covered during the program. If the students began to discuss experiences that were not related to that trip—which, of course, they would since so much had happened between the experience and the interview—the interviewer would gently move them back to memories associated with the nature center program without cueing them to the topics covered. In sum, one can learn much more about long-term impacts of a program from talking to people than scoring a survey sheet.

The majority of results used in this book come from interviews that had a specific approach to questioning. In almost all cases, visitors led the interviews and the researchers probed their responses without giving specific information about the interpretive program. Below is an example of the researchers' inquiry method during interviews:

Initial Prompts
- What kinds of things happened on the tour?
- Could you describe the parts of the tour you liked best? What parts did you like the least?
- How did _____ make you feel?
- You mentioned _____. Is there anything else I should know about that?
- Did anything about the tour strike a chord with you?
- What other things do you remember looking at or hearing about?
- What other things did the ranger talk about or point out?
- Did the ranger have a particular style or do anything that you liked or didn't like? What was it?
- Were there any main ideas or themes you think were covered during the canal tour?

Further Prompts
- What made you go on the tour?
- Did you expect anything from the tour? If so, what?
- What did you think of Lowell before you visited?

- Did you feel any differently about Lowell after the tour?
- Would you want to go on a tour like that again? Why or why not?
- Do you feel like you learned anything new? What was it?
- Have you thought about the tour since you've been home? What did you think about?
- What would you have told a friend about the tour right after you got home?
- Did you feel differently or the same about Lowell after you went on the tour? Were your understandings of the place different or the same after the tour?
- Were there any topics or information that made a connection with you or your life? How did it connect to you?

Program Specific Prompts
- Did the tour make you feel any way about the place? In other words, did it strike you as a nice place, a harsh place?
- What did you think about when you…
  …went past the factories?
  …were in the lock chamber?
  …heard about the story of the flood gate?
  …heard about the building of the canals?

Summary Prompt
- Anything else I should know? Anything you'd like to know about the study?

Answers to the interviews were then "coded" or categorized into a variety of topics or subjects that were consistent with results. For example, in almost every study, interviewees said or recalled something about the interpreter who was leading the experience. Therefore, those answers would then be "coded" as interpreter-related topics. This arduous process produced hundreds of pages of statements categorized in a variety of topics—from physical setting to personal experience related to the subject. Below is a sample of a coding summary from a qualitative study of the Yosemite Valley tram tours. The coded topic is "tangibles" that were shared by the interviewees. This sample is only one of many codes and 300 pages of statements.

Tangibles—Seeing Climbers
Seeing Climbers—Climbers Small on Rock
Document "Yosemite." Five passages, 259 characters.
> *He could point out the climbers that you couldn't even see with the naked eye. You almost had to have binoculars to see them, but he knew that they were there.*

YOSEMITE NATIONAL PARK TRAM TOUR/NPS PHOTO

He could point out where they were.
You could see, like, little ants up on the face of it.

Document "Yosemite." One passage, 91 characters.
Climbers on Half Dome. And we hopped out and took out our binoculars to take a look at them.

Document "Yosemite." One passage, 72 characters.
People just looked like small ants on the face of those big, huge things.

Document "Yosemite." One passage, 112 characters.
We went by the climbing wall, where people were climbing, you could barely see them. That was really interesting.

Document "Yosemite." Two passages, 201 characters.
It was amazing, I would never have noticed that or even known, you know, that people, uh, that there were even people, uh, up there."
To see them up there, it was like, so tiny, they were so tiny up there.

Document "Yosemite." Three passages, 282 characters.
I can't remember how many camps were there in the park, a lot, and, uh, and we, uh, you know, we were encouraged to try to locate the climbers on, you know, the sides of the rock.

Research Using Both Quantitative and Qualitative Approaches

A recent study assessing the impacts of an interpretive guided tour of a historical landmark used both qualitative and quantitative measures. This mixed-methods approach is highly popular with academics for the obvious reason that it uses different measures to acquire data. The study and its results are further explained in Chapter 2. However, this research approach is important to review for both its analysis techniques and the differences in results.

The quantitative analysis consisted of a pre-test and post-test that utilized a Likert scale to measure participants' agreement or disagreement with the tour content statements, as well as to collect demographic and contact information. Participants were asked to respond to the prompts using a Likert scale of 1–5 (1=Strongly Disagree, 2=Disagree, 3=Undecided, 4=Agree, 5=Strongly Agree). The questions consisted of statements associated with tour content. The pre-test was given to the participants during the waiting period prior to the start of the tour. The accompanying post-test was administered directly following the interpretive tour. Data was analyzed and subjected to a common quantitative process—the repeated measures T-test, using SPSS (Statistical Package for the Social Sciences) statistical software.

The qualitative portion of the study was an attempt to explore the long-term memory retention and impacts upon the same participants who completed the pre- and post-test at the tour site. The researchers used in-depth interviews to comprehend the participants' site-based interpretive experience. This particular qualitative approach is defined as phenomenology, which assesses the impact of the phenomenon (in this case, the interpretive tour). Six months following the tour, participants were contacted and interviewed (in a similar fashion as noted in this chapter). Their responses were then categorized, which helped develop major themes related to their recollections and/or impact of the tour.

The results from the two research approaches were completely different. The quantitative analysis showed statistically significant increases in knowledge regarding the tour topics. Six months later, the interviews yielded very little recollection of the topics of the tour—at least in specifics—unless the visitor had prior connections or experiences with the tour topics. This discrepancy was not a surprise to the researchers and was expected—although not to the degree that it occurred.

The findings of both approaches offer two important considerations:

- Although quantitative studies are more respected in academia, and to some extent interpretive agencies themselves, significant results using on-site approaches *do not* translate to actual knowledge gained.

- Although qualitative measures are not as accepted as "true research," the results from this strategy—in particular longitudinal approaches—can uncover key variables that actually have long-term impacts and can be important when developing successful programs.

Some people were able to do that, but not very many.
Ranger had to, uh, had to point out where people were.

Document "Yosemite." Three passages, 78 characters.
You just would not immediately have noticed.
They were there, though.

This qualitative approach produced rich information from school field trips to visitor center programs. Its use is validated by its acceptance in research journals in science education, environmental education, interpretation, and even multicultural education. And, most importantly, its results offer excellent guidance for those leading interpretive programs and wanting to achieve the most in the short amount of time allotted through this informal education process.

A Focus on Long-Term Memory
Ultimately, successful interpretation is closely associated with what it is attempting to achieve. However, the variance of desired outcomes relative to an interpretive program precludes sweeping notions of successful interpretation. Rather, success can only be measured by what is accomplished—actual or perceived—by the interpreter.

Certainly, for most interpreters, a successful outcome should be seen long after the program has ended. The challenge with this "wish" is the ability to measure such impacts when the program itself lasts 30 minutes out of an individual's 365-day year. For example, how can an interpreter know that a visitor's attitude toward redwoods has changed because of an interpretive program at Redwoods State Park? Perhaps it was the 40-minute program at the park, or it may have been the month-long special on Sequoias on the Discovery Channel, or it could have been their children's own work on a school project on redwood trees. Therefore, pinpointing an interpreter's impact in a long line of experiences may be impossible to truly assess.

However, one question that can be analyzed is how much does a participant of an interpretive program remember long after the experience? Hence, an important variable consistent in this book is visitor recollections three months to three years after the interpretive experience. Even though retention is far less "attractive" an outcome than attitude or behavior change, it is a marker that *can* be measured from an episodic event such as an interpretive program. This is not to say that an interpretive program cannot achieve important outcomes such as attitude and behavior change—it is just simply more difficult to measure.

There has been significant memory research in informal education arenas such as museum studies and school field trips. However, there is a lack of research directly associated with personal interpretive services. Since the field has not offered a great deal of literature in memory retention, the author used the field of psychology to aid in further investigating interpretation's impact on long-term retention. In particular, Endel Tulving's (1972) proposed distinction between episodic and semantic memories provides the most appropriate framework for event-specific research associated with this book.

Tulving's Long-Term Memory Theory: Remembering and Knowing
Endel Tulving is a Canadian neuroscientist and a professor emeritus at the University of Toronto. He is noted as one of the most creative and insightful theoreticians in the field of memory. In this regard, his theory of "encoding specificity" may be his most significant contribution. The theory emphasizes the fact that memories are retrieved from long-term memory by means of retrieval cues. For example, a very large number of memories stored in one's brain are not currently active, but the word "Disneyland" might instantly call to mind a trip to that amusement park. The theory of encoding specificity states that the most effective retrieval cues are those that were stored along with the memory of the experience itself. Thus, the words "amusement park" might not serve to retrieve the memory of a trip to Disneyland because, while there, the park was not specifically thought of as an "amusement park." Instead, it was thought of as Disneyland. As such, that is the cue that retrieves the appropriate memory from the vast ocean of memories that are stored in one's brain. This theory of how memories are retrieved almost seems obvious once it is explained, but it was not at all obvious before Endel Tulving explained it and then demonstrated its validity in a series of seminal studies.

Tulving's theory (1972, 1983) is based on the notion that there are two primary memory systems: *remembering* and *knowing*. According to Tulving, *remembering* entails recalled experiences and information from particular events and is considered *episodic memory*. It is a state in which images, feelings, and other context-specific details relating to a past event come to mind, such as reliving a particular episode from the past. The second system of *knowing* is a person's conceptual knowledge about the world. This knowledge of facts or events without need for recollective cues is considered *semantic memory*. His theory suggests that episodic and semantic systems are functionally independent but inclusively related in that episodic systems are embedded in semantic memory (Conway, Perfect, Anderson, Gardiner, & Cohen, 1997). According to Tulving, episodic memory is "involved in the recording and subsequent retrieval of memories of personal happenings and doings," and recalls events that are personally experienced at a specific time and place. Semantic memory is "knowledge of the world that is independent of a person's identity and past" (Tulving, 1983, p. 9). It enables an individual to recall details associated with these memories that construct a mental representation of the world. Semantic memory's content is thus abstract and relational and is associated with the meaning of verbal symbols. Tulving, along with other psychologists, suggests that early learning (related to a particular concept) is acquired and retained in episodic forms. As learning progresses, these memory representations shift from episodic to being more conceptual and hence semantic in nature (Herbert & Burt, 2004).

In relationship to interpretation, episodic memory allows individuals to recall the actual interpretive program and topic(s) and other specific information related to the event. Semantic memory enables the individual to draw in general knowledge that could be stimulated by the episodic memory. Hypothetically, information attached to the episodic recollection would assimilate into the more conceptual semantic knowledge. For example, a visitor's episodic recall of a bird of prey program that focused on the animals' adaptations could possibly assimilate into semantic knowledge that wildlife has a variety of ways to survive.

Three Variables that Aid Memory
Research related to Tulving's theoretical structure notes three important variables that can aid in episodic memory systems and, hence, ultimately increase the odds of "capture" in semantic memory. First, repeated exposure to a particular concept through different contexts has been found to aid in episodic recall and strengthen actual knowledge of the subject. This perspective is consistent with educational research examining long-term retention of knowledge taught in schools (Semb & Ellis, 1994).

A second influence on the strengthening of recall of particular concepts is its actual relevance to the individual. In order for information to become more abstract and, in turn, recalled more easily, it should be presented within the context of relevant examples. Research reports that individuals' abilities to retain information are often aided when the content is delivered in a way that is practical in nature, based on real-life experiences, and perceived as connected to their own everyday lives (Ramsden, 1997). Under such circumstances, individuals may be especially inclined to make strategic choices about which information to acquire and they may therefore be likely to expose themselves to information relevant to themselves (p. 2).

A third variable that has been found to aid in episodic systems is related to active delivery of content and concepts. There has been a growing interest in this relationship resulting in a significant volume of research in the area (Koriat, 2003). The result of much of this research has underscored the importance of actions and episodic memory performance. A better self-involvement in action events helps the rememberer to be more aware of his action and self-knowing, thereby leading to a better episodic memory.

In summary, Tulving's theory related to episodic and semantic memory systems seems to be a prudent theoretical base to analyze the long-term recollections of an interpretive program. For example, are there particular aspects of an interpretive program that enhance episodic recall? Can the potential episodic memories of such programs be assimilated into semantic memory?

A Model of Learning for Interpretation
Tulving's long-term memory theory, along with the research discussed in this book, offer a potential model of learning for interpretation. This model is

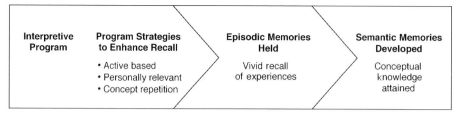

Figure 1. A Learning Model for an Interpretive Program

Canal Boat Program	Relevant Topics	Specific Recall	Knowledge Gained
	Immigration story	Lock system	Importance of
	Mill life	Francis Gate	Lowell as an
	Canal history	River's use	industrial center
			Influence of worker
			during this era

Figure 2. An Example of the Process of Learning at Lowell National Historical Park

couched in episodic or semantic memory systems, which, as posited previously, is the most pragmatic approach to view impacts of a one-time event such as an interpretive program. The model (Figure 1) is based on the idea that an interpretive event offers a set of experiences that would relate to one or more of the three variables that enhance episodic memory systems (active experiences, repetitive content, and information relevant to participants).

Figure 2 is an example of the use of this learning model. The subject of the model is the Lowell National Historical Park canal boat program. The interpretive tour offers topics that include the industrial revolution, mill operations, and ways in which Lowell has changed over the years. This program offers experiences that many of the visitors could relate to directly or indirectly. The visitor connections developed during the boat program aided in vivid episodic memories. These recollections, in turn, enhanced the potential for semantic memories and conceptual learning.

In an attempt to further illustrate the use of the learning model, suggestions for other potential program strategies during the canal program are offered below:

Active-Based Experiences: Since the canal program was primarily a didactic tour, more boat "responsibilities" could be assigned to the visitors. This could include aiding the interpreter in citing key points along the way or offering their own ideas of what they are seeing prior to the guide's explanation. This approach could even include songs that were reflective of the mill era.

LOWELL NATIONAL HISTORIC PARK CANAL BOAT PROGRAM/AUTHOR PHOTO

Concept Repetition: This strategy would be enhanced in this program through the elimination of some of the content to enable more focused and repetitive discussion related to the primary theme of the role of Lowell in the Industrial Revolution and the importance of immigrants in this story.

Personally Relevant: This program succeeds in attaining vivid episodic recall through personally relevant information. However, this approach could have been further developed by giving participants opportunities to share their own connections to the park. Visitor stories shared through this format would have potentially motivated other stories from participants, enabling more personal connections to be developed.

The simplicity of the proposed learning model reflects the episodic nature of interpretation. Its linear structure emphasizes the longitudinal impact that must be assessed to evaluate the "success" of learning. However, the program strategies offered in this model can only be implemented within the duration of the interpretive program, which is, in many cases, less than an hour. Therefore, the types of experiences offered in the second stage of the model are crucial. With the Lowell example, personally relevant topics can potentially be a successful approach. For other programs that are covered in this book, other strategies have enabled long-term retention.

Therefore, this book offers a wide range of programs, experiences, and methods that include one or more of the program strategies associated with the learning model that can aid in memory retention of an interpretive experience.

Summary

The results offered in this book are a testament to the past leaders of interpretation, who have assumed that our profession does make a difference. It is a record of "tried and true" interpretive strategies that have made an impact months and/or years after the experience. Have visitors changed behavior? Are they better citizens for experiencing these types of programs? We *hope* so, and now we *know* that our programs have a lasting impact. And for someone who has always been in the back of the room shouting, "Prove it!" it is a start.

2 Creating a Successful Interpretive Program

The use of interpretation as a form of communication has been prevalent throughout the 20th century. The roots of this field can be traced to individuals such as John Muir, who is noted as being the first to use the term *interpret* in the context that still embodies the philosophy of interpretation: "I'll interpret the rocks, learn the language of flood, storm and the avalanche. I'll acquaint myself with the glaciers and wild gardens, and get as near the heart of the world as I can" (Macintosh, 1986).

The goal set out by Muir is noted as one of the earliest forms of interpretation. His quest was for a deeper understanding of the earth, an important aspect of today's interpretation. Muir's writings and observations of our natural resources were accompanied by those of others such as John Burroughs and J. D. Whitney. They were pioneers in helping others learn about the environment around them. However, it wasn't until the early 1900s that any true form of public awareness about natural areas came to exist, when Enos Mills, an inn keeper in Colorado, helped to work toward the establishment of Rocky Mountain National Park. Mills also promoted and led guided hikes through the area. His goal was to increase the appreciation of the park's natural values. The term "nature guide" began with Mills' work.

John Muir (with Theodore Roosevelt), Enos Mills, and Freeman Tilden

For the following decades, the title of *nature guide* began to be replaced by *naturalist* or nature *interpreter*. These individuals related pertinent and interesting natural history to the visitors who came to their park, reserve, or nature center. A hallmark for the interpretive field was Freeman Tilden's book *Interpreting Our Heritage*, written in 1957. It was this work that began to shape the goals and philosophies of interpretation. The field saw a steady increase in popularity during the 1960s and early 1970s at the state and national park levels in particular. Today, the profession involves tens of thousands of interpreters in virtually every community in this country. These positions can be found in museums, zoos, aquaria, camps, private industry, and federal, state, and local agencies.

Essential Ingredients to a Successful Interpretive Program

The evolution of interpretation has brought about a variety of elements that can be considered essential for a successful interpretive program. Tilden's principles of interpretation laid out in *Interpreting Our Heritage* are still considered essential for accomplishing program objectives in interpretation:

1. Any interpretation that does not somehow relate what is being displayed or described to something within the personality or experience of the visitor will be sterile.
2. Information, as such, is not Interpretation. Interpretation is revelation based upon information. But they are entirely different things. However, all interpretation includes information.
3. Interpretation is an art, which combines many arts, whether the materials presented are scientific, historical, or architectural. Any art is in some degree teachable.
4. The chief aim of Interpretation is not instruction, but provocation.
5. Interpretation should aim to present a whole rather than a part, and must address itself to the whole man rather than any phase.

6. Interpretation addressed to children should not be a dilution of the presentation to adults, but should follow a fundamentally different approach.

Another set of general characteristics outlined by Sam Ham (1992) have influenced interpreters' notion of what successful interpretation should entail. These four "qualities" have been noted as essential for success in almost every personal interpretation program:

- Interpretation is enjoyable
- Interpretation is relevant
- Interpretation is organized
- Interpretation has a theme

The training manual for National Association for Interpretation's Certified Interpretive Guide program is organized into five general sections: a) overview of interpretation, b) knowledge of audience, c) knowledge of resource, d) program development, and e) program delivery. These variables are the basis for one of the most aggressive training endeavors in interpretation, which has achieved worldwide recognition since its inception in 2000.

The National Park Service, through its Interpretive Development Program (IDP), has established a process that the agency suggests can reflect successful interpretive experiences. An interpretive program should create an opportunity for the audience to form its own intellectual and emotional connections with meanings or significance inherent in the resource, and it would provide a clear focus for its connection with the resource(s).

The Process for the Interpretive Development Program

- Select a tangible place, object, person, or event
- Identify intangible meanings
- Identify universal concepts
- Identify audience
- Develop a theme statement
- Use interpretive methods to develop opportunities for connections to meanings
- Organize opportunities for connections and cohesively develop an idea

In an effort to further clarify and validate elements of successful interpretation, a multiple case study of five national parks was conducted by the author. The results of this study support key philosophical and theoretical tenets upheld and promoted by the interpretive profession. Specifically, organizations such as NAI and NPS, and their associated training programs, are conveying variables that interpreters interviewed for this study believe can lead to successful interpretive experiences. These strategies include making connections with the visitor, offering innovative techniques, and meeting basic program needs.

Outline of NAI's Certified Interpretive Guide Training Program

I. Overview
- NAI's Definition of Interpretation
- Principles of Interpretation
- Understanding Social Marketing
- Weaving a Story of Tangible Things, Intangible Ideas, and Universal Concepts

II. Knowledge of the Audience
- Understanding and Applying Maslow's Hierarchy
- Understanding Learning Styles
- Audience Evaluation

III. Knowledge of the Resource
(note: NAI's CIG program is not resource-based; instead, the content focuses on application of theory, research, and techniques so that the training program can be used in any resource setting)
- Offer Balanced Information
- Design a Research Plan

IV. Program Development
- Interpretation is Purposeful (serves the mission of the organization)
- Interpretation is Organized
- Interpretation is Enjoyable
- Interpretation is Thematic
- Interpretation is Relevant
- Interpretation Depends on You (the interpreter makes the connection between the interests of the audience and the meanings inherent in the resource, and as such, must keep developing as a professional)

V. Program Delivery
- Creating a Program Outline
- Questioning and Response Strategies
- Using Gimmicks and Gadgets
- Verbal and Nonverbal Communication Strategies
- Ways to Interface with Visitors
- Informal Interpretation
- Authority of the Resource
- Self-Evaluation

Do What We Say, Not What We Do!

The campfire program started well enough. The interpreter was gracious and personable when folks came to the amphitheater. "How are you tonight?" asked the ranger. "Are you camping here or staying in the lodge?" These questions, along with other inquiries about their park visit, helped break the ice and many of the arriving participants were eager to share their answers. Then the program began, and as if a switch was turned on (or off in this instance) the ranger went full-speed into an hour-long lecture on bears. The audience had disappeared, interaction of the kind that warmed up the participants was long gone—no one was heard from again, except the interpreter.

This scenario happened all too often as I spent my sabbatical visiting national parks and learning more about what interpreters believed were important factors to successful programs and observing to see if these same variables were utilized in the parks' programs. I had the opportunity to interview 36 interpreters (both field level and supervisors) from five different national parks: Yellowstone, Great Smoky Mountains, Shenandoah, Cuyahoga, and George Washington Carver. *All* of these folks said that an interpretive program should relate or "connect" with the visitor and be "dynamic" in style.

Unfortunately, in the public interpretive programs I observed at these same parks, this passion to connect with the visitor was absent. At one park, for example, I observed a wildflower "walk" that had the audience standing over one plant for 15 minutes while the interpreter droned on about this particular plant species. He lost the children (and half of the adults) in the group within two minutes of his oration.

Hence, this study found an important paradox. What we say we want a successful interpretive program to be isn't always what we do. In particular, the interpreters I talked with wanted programs that related their topic to their constituents. But the programs I saw didn't make those connections. Rarely did an interpreter interject into the presentation and ask something like, "So, do you have this type of plant in your neck of the woods?" or, "What would you do if you saw a bear on the trail?" The lack of a two-way dialogue limited the actual knowledge the interpreter could have regarding his/her audience (i.e., emotional, cognitive, and/or physical state at the time of the interpretive experience), debilitating the chances for visitor connections.

The omission of a two-way dialogue runs counter to the basic premise of both the National Association for Interpretation and the National Park Service's goals of visitor connections. As David Larsen (2002) states:

> We need to know more about our audiences! Accurate and up-to-date knowledge of audience perceptions, the meanings they bring to our resources, the way they make personal connections, and how interpretive experiences affect them over time are tremendously valuable…. The Interpretive Development Program is encouraging interpreters when they

> informally encounter audiences to ask questions like, "What did you hope to find here? What do you hope your children will take from this experience? If you had my job what would you tell people?" (p. 22)

The clear emphasis on promoting connections with the visitor and enhancing meanings they acquire from their park visit counters with the one-way communications I consistently found in observing park programs. Therefore, interpreters should look at an interpretive approach that is based on a constructivist learning theory that promotes interactions between the learner and teacher, or in this case, the participant and the interpreter.

A major theme in the constructivist framework is that learning is an active process in which the learner (in this case, the visitor) construct new ideas or concepts based upon their current or past knowledge. The learner selects and transforms information, constructs hypotheses, and makes decisions, relying on a cognitive structure to do so. The interpreter and visitor would therefore engage in an active dialogue with the interpreter presenting information that matches with the visitor's current state of understanding. Therefore, the interpreter, at times, would be a facilitator rather than an orator.

So back to the campfire program: If the ranger used a constructivist approach, many of the visitors would actually have had an opportunity to give input into the program or would have been able to ask questions about one or more of the topics the interpreter brought to the program. In essence, a constructivist-style campfire program would have led to a dialogue with the participants. Understandably, this direction would be a more challenging interpretive style, but one that, in the end, may produce more meaningful connections with the visitors and hence a more successful program.

Tried and True Strategies to Successful Interpretive Programs
So how do the tenets of successful interpretation stand up to the actual impact of traditional interpretive programs? What strategies, experiences, or methods seem to offer the greatest bang for the buck? This section offers a glimpse of five different interpretive experiences and how they impacted their participants.

Lowell National Historical Park Canal Boat Tour
The history of America's Industrial Revolution is commemorated at Lowell National Historical Park. Exhibits and tours tell the story of the Northeast's transition from farm to factory, chronicle immigrant labor history, and trace industrial technology. An important part of the interpretation of this site is canal boat tours that wind through the heart of the mills and waterways located in the city of Lowell, Massachusetts. Participants travel along a canal, float through a lock chamber, and tour a part of the Merrimack River. Topics offered by the interpreter include the industrial revolution, mill operations, the role of the river and canals in powering the mills, immigrants, laborers,

natural history, historic preservation, and ways in which Lowell has changed over the years.

Participants of the Lowell canal boat programs were interviewed six months following their experience. Their responses were consistently formed by the connections they made to the mills and its history. These connections were based on their own personal experiences with mills or related topics.

> *We actually had a neighbor when I was a child who was a mill girl. So I had lots of stories about the mill girls. … A lot, you know, family members, grandmothers, great-grandmothers, not all of whom I've met, but I've heard the stories throughout the years.*
>
> *One of my grandmothers worked in the mill. … I really wanted my daughter to see and understand some of the history of our family or it will die with me.*

Food for Thought

The Lowell canal boat program is a traditional venue that enables the interpreter to "lecture" to the passengers for the duration of the 45-minute tour. Much more information was "given" to the participants than what was recalled. However, despite the monologue structure—or because of it—visitors "captured" information that made direct connections to their own lives. Freeman Tilden's first principle of relating to the visitor is certainly supported by these results.

My granddaughter wanted to know if there was anybody in our family who had been in these mills. And we said, "Yeah, that's part of our heritage, too, is the mills." … My wife was the working side of the mill, and my father's people were the owners' side of the mill.

My family grew up there. So it's sort of in a way sentimental for me. … I know from past trips I've had, my nieces and nephews who were born in Lowell, were very young when they left here, so they enjoyed it because they felt the same way. They were learning more about their family.

The relevancy of Lowell's history to the participants created vivid recall that included general ideas and/or knowledge attached to participants' recollections of the interpretive experience. Ideas and concepts essential to the mission of Lowell National Historical Park are found in the responses of the visitors long after the boat ride.

You really got a sense of where people came from for this mill work and how it grew up around Lowell, and what a really important place Lowell has been in the whole history of the Industrial Revolution.

The significant role that Lowell played in the beginning of manufacturing in our country affected not just Lowell but became a forerunner for the rest and a model for many other parts of the country as well.

You walk away with an appreciation of all the sacrifices that people made and appreciate the hardship of the people and what they had to do to bring us forward economically in this country.

Denali National Park Dog Sled Program
As one of the largest national parks, Denali National Park contains hundreds of thousands of acres of wilderness. It also can lay claim to one of the oldest running interpretive programs in the country—the dog sled demonstration. Since 1921, sled dogs have been used to help patrol and access much of the park. In the early years of the park, dogs outnumbered park personnel. Visitors began seeking out the dog kennels at Denali as early as the 1930s. Each year, an estimated 50,000 visitors attend the interpretive program to learn about the use of sled dogs in Denali.

Eight to 10 months following participation in the dog sled program, visitors were contacted by researchers to learn what they retained from the interpretive experience. Many of their responses were devoted to information still vividly recalled from the 30-minute program. A variety of general to specific information that was part of the interpretive talk was offered through the interviews.

DENALI NATIONAL PARK DOG SLED PROGRAM/AUTHOR PHOTO

They explained about [rangers] using [dogs] in the winter to patrol not only for skiers that come in, but poachers.

I remember that they were using them since the park opened. At first it was the only way they could get around.

The dogs were the first order of transportation and it drew the country together as far as their mail system went.

Food for Thought
Interpreters that led these dog sled demonstrations had concerns that their own interpretive messages may have been lost due to the presence of the sled dogs. To their surprise, the dogs' relationship with the interpreters actually was the key to getting across their mission in a lasting way.

There are various possibilities for the vivid retention of the program by the Denali visitors. However, one variable found through this research that was a clear "conduit" of recollection was the connections the people made with the dogs—even after only a 30-minute exposure to them.

She had a deep respect for people who care for animals. I mean we just recently got a new puppy and so I understand the dedication and the amount of work it takes, especially when you are dealing with that number of dogs.

Very few places anymore have a relationship with the animals in which they contribute more than just being pets. But the animals did actually pull things and help us do farming. So for me it was an opportunity to see a case in which animals and humans are still working together to do something that needs to get done.

Tusayan Museum Tour and Walk
Grand Canyon National Park's Tusayan Museum provides a glimpse of Pueblo Indian life at the Grand Canyon. A small museum offers "Glimpses of the Past," a popular museum tour and walk interpreting the artifacts and culture of an 800-year-old Pueblo Indian ruin discovered near the south rim of the Grand Canyon. The tour is offered on a daily basis, with the first part of the experience touring the museum followed by an exploration of the adjacent ruins.

Ten months following their visit to the museum, visitors seemed to make individual connections with the Indian culture both inside the museum and outside in the ruins. Their interviews also demonstrated vivid content retention associated with tour topics.

I am amazed at how they [Pueblo Indians] lived and how they survived and I compare it to our cushy lifestyle and I don't believe I could make it. I think I would have probably thrown myself off the cliff.

How did these people manage to live in these little places? You stretch out on the

TUSAYAN RUINS/NPS PHOTO

*floor and from one end of the building to the other and whole families are in
there. And then you find yourself wondering how anyone even survived in the
area because in June it was rather warm. And not a stream and you've got to find
water. You've got to find a way to grow food.*

Many of the visitors referenced an artist's painting inside the museum that helped
them conceptualize aspects of the Pueblo Indian culture. Visitors were able to
imagine both the structure of the original building as it may have appeared and the
daily lives of the human inhabitants.

*Well it looked like low walls of stone. It
looked like ruins in the sense that there
was nothing more than about a foot
high. But you could see the pattern of
rooms in the stones on the ground.
And I remember thinking that a lot of
people lived in a relatively small place.*

Food for Thought
Although the Tusayan Museum is a
small facility, the large painting that
is the focal point of the museum
exhibits became a "portal" to enter
when the visitors explored the
adjacent ruins.

*Then I remember thinking that I was really glad I saw the diagrams and
descriptions inside the museum because it allowed me to visualize what the ruins
would have looked like.*

The Haleakala Star Program
Haleakala National Park was established on the island of Maui to preserve the
outstanding features of Haleakala Crater. Later additions to the park gave
protection to the unique and fragile ecosystems and rare biotic species of
Kipahulu Valley, the scenic pools along 'Obe'o Gulch, and the coast. The higher
elevations of Haleakala offer some of the best opportunities in the world for star
gazing. So, not surprisingly, astronomy programs are a mainstay for interpretation
at the park. Participants of these star gazing programs lie in the middle of a
mountain meadow as two interpreters offer facts and stories related to the major
constellations and the secrets of Polynesian navigation.

Two years after one of these programs, visitors were interviewed to learn what
they recalled from an hour on their backs, gazing at the Hawaiian sky. The
information given through these interviews represented impressive retention of
the subject matter related to the stars and their stories.

*The aspect that I remember was the Polynesian names for the constellations and
then how navigators were able to determine longitude, which was a problem
because they didn't have clocks or chronometers. And then they associated
Polynesian myths for the formation of the constellations.*

*There was a local figure who they worshipped over the generations who saved his
wife or girlfriend from a sea monster or something. And that his story was told in*

SUNSET AT HALEAKALA/AUTHOR PHOTO

the sky through generations. They passed on [the story] through the generations through astronomy.

A unique aspect to the Haleakala star program was the tandem approach with a ranger sharing astronomy and a native Hawaiian sharing local stories associated with the constellations. This combination certainly made an impact.

Food for Thought
Whether it was the novelty of lying in a field on a mountain top in Hawaii or the dramatic clarity of the night sky, the content and stories from this hour-long interpretive program were still imbedded with the visitor *two years* after the program.

What I remember most about it was one gentleman talking about the technical aspects of astronomy and another talking about Hawaiian lore as it pertains to astronomy. And that was very interesting because I figure we should go up there and go star gazing and see the stars. But then there was a Hawaiian woman who put the Hawaiian lore with it. It was very special. So that was really good.

I remember the ranger pointed to different constellations and the native related stories and how they made up stories to go along with the constellation. And one of the stories was about a little boy who went swimming and there was something about the time of year when the sharks were in the water. And so they were relating something about the orientation of the stars with perhaps a dangerous time to go swimming because of the sharks. It is funny because I remembered that story pretty clearly for a long time.

Jefferson National Expansion Museum Tours
At the base of the St. Louis Arch is the Jefferson National Expansion Memorial Museum. Thousands of visitors visit the museum on a daily basis. The exhibits are dedicated to the history of Lewis and Clark and the western expansion of the United States. In an attempt to highlight aspects of the museum, the park offers interpreter-led tours of the exhibits, which focus on aspects of the Lewis and Clark expedition. The 30-minute tours use a variety of visual aids, props, demonstrations, and audience interaction.

Six months after the tours, visitors were interviewed to assess what they recalled pertaining to the 30-minute experiences. The richest recollection was by far the props and demonstrations. In fact, the first recollection at the start of the interview for most participants contained references to props used by the ranger.

He showed the raccoon-skin hats that Lewis and Clark wore and we got to wear these moccasins from the Indians, I think. And I got to wear a suit that was all itchy. I kind of remember the soldier one. It kind of had some metal buttons and it was pretty sturdy. It wasn't like a normal suit.

I remember she came in with her cart and she had some things that she was going to use for the talk, like different parts of the uniforms that they would have used. I think she had some type of Indian wear.

Yeah, he demonstrated how flint makes a spark with a piece of flint and a piece of metal, striking the one on the other.

Actually, the reason I remember this stuff is because we got to see the rope and they demonstrated what it was like to pull it and then we got to see the replicas of the money. And because we were able to touch and feel this stuff, that is why it sticks out in my mind.

An important "conduit" for retention of the use of the props was the children of the participants. Many of the studies included in this book have shown the influence the children had on adults' recall of interpretive programs. Virtually anything that a son or daughter would show interest or enthusiasm in was then passed to the parents.

My younger son was excited about being able to touch the props and carry around the props and show them to the adults.

Make Sure the Program Matches Your Mission

Not all of the studies conducted on interpretive programs found results that matched the wishes of the sponsoring agency. In particular, one program that found little in the way of findings that would be pleasing to the program's mission was conducted at a historical site in southern Indiana. As historic sites go, the West Baden Springs Hotel (WBSH) is matched by few. The hotel, constructed in the early 1900s, was considered the eighth wonder of the world with a free-standing, open-air lobby that wasn't matched by size until the construction of the Houston Astrodome. Throughout the past century, the WBSH was used as a hotel and spa, Jesuit seminary, and a culinary school, and later was vacated and left to the elements, falling into a state of ill repair.

In 1992, Historic Landmarks Foundation of Indiana began stabilizing and renovating the historical site. During the renovation period, the foundation offered tours of the hotel, highlighting the glamorous history of the structure and educating visitors about the preservation and reconstruction of the WBSH in all its details. In fact, the primary mission of the interpretive tours was to highlight the importance of the foundation and its work to restore the old hotel.

Eight months following their participation in these tours, visitors offered general retention about the large lobby and the architecture. But not one of the individuals recalled what foundation or organization was responsible for the renovations and its importance to the project.

So what were the reasons for the interpretive program not living up to the mission statement?

Was it the tour guide?

Our guide was very wonderful…. He was very knowledgeable and it was quite evident that he was enjoying what he was doing.

No—high marks for the guides. Was it the "tangible"—the hotel itself?

The wonderful domed room…that was magnificent. Everything about it was quite impressive.

No—good recollections of the architecture and the impressive dome.

The "basics" of the program seemed to be present, including an enthusiastic interpreter and an impressive tangible—the hotel itself. So why didn't visitors recall the importance of the Historic Landmarks Foundation of Indiana (or even its name)? Simply, the tour never infused the agency's role during the talk and hence had no opportunity for the visitors to make connections between themselves and the agency or the project itself. It was a no-show at its own party.

So what is the moral of the results of this study? Make sure you interpret what you wish for, or it may be a wish that will never come true.

I was happy for my son to get a little bit of, to be able to be involved in the costumes, and he was excited about it, and I think it got him going a little bit for history.

She was passing things around for the kids to, like, feel and see how heavy things were. I think she passed around, like, a fur pelt to the kids. She passed it around for everyone, but the kids were very interested in that kind of stuff, hands-on things. I'm thinking there was a blanket or a fur something she put on the kids to see how heavy it was.

He passed around a lot of things. I just remember they [kids] were interested in it. It was a good way to get them to pay attention. I know they passed around some clothes. And I think the kids might have tried some on. I think they passed around some kind of musket.

The Bottom Line

Each of the previous case studies has several important elements in common. First, all of the programs can be considered traditional person-to-person interpretation. Second, each is a staple of the respective park's visitor experience. Third, all of them offer evidence of long-term impact, whether it was intellectual, emotional, or attitudinal. Finally, each of the programs had a particular "hook" that aided in the connection of the message to the visitor. For Lowell, it was the personal relevance of the mill history to those aboard the canal boats. At Denali, it was the dogs and their interactions with the rangers. The Tusayan Museum's painting created the threshold for their visitors. At Haleakala, it was the sheer awe of the night sky over Hawaii, and for the Jefferson National Museum it was the props supplied by the interpreter.

These connections take us full circle to the elements of successful interpretation:

Food for Thought

As an interpreter many years ago, the author viewed family-oriented programs as the most difficult to pull off successfully. On one end are kids surrounding you like flies, while parents tend to hang back and enjoy a few minutes of break from their children. Some days, it would feel as if I were a planet with inner and outer rings. However, research from these types of programs supports the idea that this chaotic variance actually sets up a successful vehicle for long-term program retention. In particular, the fathers and mothers remember program information and experiences if they successfully connect with their kids. So, in the case of family audiences, it may be beneficial to take on the inner ring and the outer ring will follow.

- For Freeman Tilden, it was his first principle: "Any interpretation that does not somehow relate what is being displayed or described to something within the personality or experience of the visitor will be sterile."

- For the National Association for Interpretation, it is creating both emotional and intellectual connections to something within the audience's frame of reference.

- For the National Park Service it is "using interpretive methods to develop opportunities for connections to meanings."

However it is said, a "successful" program *must connect with the visitor*. Hence, a primary task of any interpreter is to find what tangible or intangible aspect of the program can make that connection. If found, their use can have lasting effects.

3

Large Group Interpretation

The Use of Lectures and Campfire Talks

Park visitors are keen to utilize evening hours at a campfire program. People gather at hotels, lodges, and campgrounds, join in community singing, and listen to musical and educational programs. A prime feature of all these programs is a talk by a naturalist or historian, who explains various scientific or historic features of the park. Both motion pictures and lantern slides are used for illustrations. Interest and attendance have brought about improved equipment in the form of outdoor amphitheaters providing comfortable seats and suitable projection equipment.

Lectures vary widely in subject and method of presentation so as to fit location and type of audience. Around a small campfire in a campground, the program is very informal, whereas at central locations, the presentation may be more formal and with less opportunity for questions from the audience. Special animal lectures are given in several parks at the bear-feeding platforms. Dependable information on animal life, given with live specimens as illustrations, has proved very successful.

—Recreational Use of Land in the United States, 1938

Since the inception of interpretation, large group presentations have been a staple of the profession. Long before Tilden's *Interpreting Our Heritage* and decades prior to the 1938 mandate for their recreational use, campfires and other large gatherings were used for cultural, natural, and resource management messages. Below are excerpts of notes from federal agencies depicting their use in the early 1900s:

> The University of California extension division inaugurated a lecture series in memory of Professor Joseph LeConte at Yosemite in 1919 and continued it through 1923. Speakers the first summer included Professor Willis L. Jepson of the university on botany; William Frederic Bade, John Muir's literary executor, on Muir; Professor A.L. Kroeber of the university on local Indians; and Francois Emile Matthes of the U.S. Geological Survey on geology. Matthes stayed in the park, giving additional talks in the public camps and at Sierra Club campfires.
>
> After the turn of the century some improvement in the quality of public presentations was evident. The Wylie Camping Company, which housed Yellowstone visitors in tents, recruited teachers who gave lectures and campfire programs while performing other duties. (Mackintosh, 1986)

Hence, the original technique to convey resource information was through lectures and campfire programs, and they certainly are still important parts of many parks' interpretive strategies.

The Orchestra Leader

There is clear evidence that large presentations contribute to further understanding of resource information and can impact attitudes to some degree. The first step to conducting programs that can make a difference is to know key variables or techniques that an interpreter should display while offering such presentations.

Leadership: From the outset of a program, the visitor needs to know that the interpreter has the ability, confidence, and comfort in leading a group. Understandably, this variable comes from experience but must be conveyed so that the message of the program is not hindered.

Affection: This term conjures the notion that, prior to an evening campfire, everyone must embrace in a group hug—not exactly. It is the idea that when an interpreter presents subject matter, there is a clear indication that he or she not only cares about the topic, but also the people. In almost all the studies associated with this book, the interpreter clearly enjoyed and had a passion for the topic. However, many programmers lacked that same interest for the audience— something that resource site visitors can pick up on very quickly. If they see that the interpreter lacks interest in them, then their own motivation for connections to the topic and interpreter will be in jeopardy.

Clarity: Knowing material well is quite different from being able to present it clearly. Again, in most cases, the interpreter may know his or her topic, but if it is not clearly explained to the audience, then a successful program will be in doubt.

Connecting the "What" with "Them": The theme to this book and to the research herein is making a connection to the audience. Too many large programs completely abandon attempts to learn something about the audience that could help them with their presentation. Simple questions woven through a program only requiring a raise of hands could aid an interpreter in presenting topics. Similar to one-on-one interpretation, this technique "drops the safety net," but the more personal connections made—even in a large group setting—the better the chances for long-term impact.

Emotional Presence—Since it is the interpreter versus "the masses," successful presentation requires the use of voice inflection, gestures, and movements to elicit and maintain attention and to stimulate visitors' emotions. Like other performers, interpreters must, above all else, convey a strong sense of presence and focused energy. Some can do this by being overtly enthusiastic, animated, or witty, while others accomplish the same effect with a quieter, more serious and intense, but equally engaging style. The ability to stimulate strong positive emotions in participants separates the competent from the outstanding interpreter.

The Path Not to Take

It is probably one of the most historical sites for a campfire program: Mammoth Hot Springs, Yellowstone National Park. A crowd of 100 or so was seated to watch an evening program on elk that began promptly at 8:30 p.m. The temperature was 45 degrees and dropping fast. The program started with a few light-hearted anecdotes on wildlife sightings of the day and some promotion of the newsletter that each car receives at the gate house when entering the park. Following the "warm up," the interpreter showed a *one-hour* slide show that had people beginning to leave at about 9:00 p.m. In fact, the author was so cold from sitting still that long (temperatures were now at 40 degrees), he departed the program at 9:30 with the leader still preaching about elk to a hearty group of about 30 folks.

You are the Conductor—It can be easy to begin a presentation and become lost in the transference of the topic to the people, who quickly become a faceless blur. But a master interpreter keeps up with the rhythm of the audience. Like a

Making Connections at 20 Miles Per Hour
(Excerpts from an interpretive tram tour of Yosemite Valley)

…In your own lives, how many have had experience with floods? What was that like for you? Was that a beautiful experience? I see some shaking heads. How many have experienced fire, either wildfire or house fire? Was that a beautiful experience for you? No again. How many have experienced an earthquake? Was that a beautiful experience for you? These are disasters, dynamic processes we refer to as disasters. Well, take a look at one of the most beautiful disasters anywhere in the world. Yosemite Valley is a result of all those dynamic processes combined. All those things combine here…

…What's one of the dynamic forces each of us deals with, especially as we get older? Gravity. Nowhere is that more evident than at Rocky Point, one of most active rock fall zones anywhere in Yosemite National Park. In 1996, one and a half tons of debris came down at once, points out where can see it. Such an active rock fall zone because [there are] lots of cracks and fissures in rock up there, lots of freeze-thaw action as well. That action loosens up the rocks. These rocks come down in all different sizes and shapes. You can take a look at some as big as houses. You can imagine you wouldn't want to be on this tram when one and a half tons of debris came down. That's gravity, always at work, always a dynamic force in Yosemite...

…Hard to ignore a 3,000-foot vertical cliff rising to the right. A spiritual icon for the Native Americans, El Capitan rises 3,000 feet straight up from the valley floor. Some of you are from Indiana. Have you stood next to the Sears Tower? How do you think that compares to El Capitan? It would take two and a half Sears Towers to make up El Capitan. It's deceptive, standing at this angle and looking at it, but it's over 3,000 feet…

…Great question. The question was whether there's any concern about climbers' impact on El Capitan. Certainly, there is. At many places, climbers are still drilling into rock. We don't allow that here at Yosemite anymore, although we used to. Now we encourage different climbing, where the lead climber places protection and following climber removes it as they go up and take them with them. So the only impact on rock is chalk from hands, and that washes off in next rainfall. So how many of you are ready for that challenge? I see a few hands…

conductor, it is an obligation to pull into the presentation those who may be waning or calm those who might be discontented. In essence, large presentations are analogous to conducting sections of an orchestra, with the conductor making sure all are on the same page.

Tried and Proven Large Interpretive Programs

The following are five case studies of large group interpretive experiences—from campfires to tram tours—that have been studied for long-term visitor impacts. Each has a variety of techniques, topics, and ranger-influenced recollections that offer evidence that large programs offer successful outcomes.

Brown County State Park Lecture Series
During the fall, Brown County State Park, a large state park in southern Indiana, offers several evening visitor center presentations. The goals of one of these programs are to make visitors aware of the natural history and life patterns of the white-tailed deer. In particular, the program studied for this book focused on animals' adaptations for survival and their impact on the region's food web. It included a 30-minute slide presentation, a 15-minute discussion led by the interpreter, and a "hands-on" period at the end of the program that enabled participants to touch and feel white-tailed deer artifacts. The hour-long program took place inside the park's nature center.

Two years following the program, participants of the program were contacted

BROWN COUNTY STATE PARK LECTURE SERIES/JAMES FARMER

to learn what, if anything, they remembered about the program. Four themes emerged from the analysis. Recollections related to 1) visual cues, 2) novel experiences, 3) interpreter-related actions, and 4) active involvement.

Visual Recollections: The participants remembered visual images related specifically to seeing slides of deer: "I remember a slide of…not a nest, but where they bedded down," and, "They took a picture downward so you could see, like, a mama and a baby together in a, like, a bedding type thing." Another representative response was: "I can see the picture of the deer with his big ears looking at me."

Novel Recollections: In a second category of recall, participants noted aspects of the program as being novel or unusual, or that drew their attention. Antlers and the other "touchable items" were a consistent response related to this theme: "It's not very often that you get to touch antlers and things like that."

Interpreter-Related Recollections: Respondents offered vivid responses related to the interpreter:

> *She was just very good, so I think one of the best things of having a good program in a recreational facility or park is having a good interpreter.*

Another response related to the interpreter's impact on their children:

> *But I thought it was just really interesting that she was able to keep it entertaining and yet put in scientific information like that without being boring. Where the kids thought, "Oh man, Mom and Dad are dragging us to this boring thing," and they were not bored in the least.*

Food for Thought

Two years following an interpretive program, this study found that individuals could recall extensive details of the program they attended. In particular, aspects of the interpreter (including personality traits and teaching techniques) and experiential parts of the program seemed to elicit the most vivid recollections.

Active-Involvement Recollections. The richest description of recalled memories related to active involvement. For example, participants recalled a hearing exercise that was conducted that involved all of the program participants cupping their ears to demonstrate hearing adaptations of deer.

> *I remembered we stood around, we cupped our hands around our ears and turned them around to give the effect of deer listening to different things at different angles.*

One participant noted that the activity was used back at their home following the program:

I have a hearing loss in both of my ears. So I use that all the time now. But all of my family still do that sometimes; cup our ears and hear and stuff.

Another active aspect of the program recalled was the passing around of objects:

[My children] got to hold and see the different antlers and skulls of different deer that had, you know, died and stuff, and they were truly excited.

Denali Visitor Center Program
On a daily basis, Denali National Park offers evening multimedia presentations in its visitor center. These programs are normally full to capacity which means approximately 150 folks listening to the topic of the night. The program assessed for this book focused its subject matter on the premier wildlife of the park— moose, caribou, grizzlies, and Dall sheep. The interpreter was a seasoned veteran who had command of the room within seconds. Her program techniques included "conversation" with the audience, a slide presentation on the animals, story telling and opportunities prior to and following the presentation to touch animal skins and antlers.

Two years after the 40-minute presentation, visitors were contacted and interviewed regarding their recollection of the evening program. The most consistent and vivid recollection tended to be the ability of the audience to touch and pick up the antlers and furs associated with animals that the interpreter was going to cover in her presentation.

Food for Thought

The visitor program was led by a master interpreter who had an excellent presence, interacted with the audience well and conveyed her message by interweaving natural history of Denali animals with her own life stories. And yet, with these variables in place, the most vivid recollection represents one of the most important constants of this book—if they can touch it, they will retain it.

We did see some skins. And the kids go crazy for that because they like to feel the nice fur. This way they can touch it. Sometimes they showed bones also which you can find out in the field if you are lucky enough because they dissolve into nothing after a short period of time.

And they had a lot of different horns or antlers from different animals and stuff. And I remember they had moose horns and you know people were trying to lift it of course, couldn't. [chuckles]. And some of the kids were trying to, because they had them set up on the stage, you know, which was kind of cool. It gives you an

The Story of Ranger Bob

(Excerpt from Denali Visitor Center Program)

Since I've been a ranger, one of the questions I get is why I became a ranger. And it goes back to that trip I took with my dad and family when I was 11 years old. See, I went to a ranger program, much like this one. And that ranger told me a story, a story about Ranger Bob. Anyone heard of Ranger Bob? He is a legendary, legendary ranger, and one that passes down all kinds of lessons to the rangers of today. Now I'm going to share that with you.

Ranger Bob was one of those rangers that goes out and looks at the trails, makes sure there weren't any trees that had fallen and everything was safe for you visitors. So he was walking the trail. Now this day Ranger Bob wasn't doing what we always tell you guys to do: Make human noise when you're out on the trail. Well, Ranger Bob was thinking about all these things he had to do. So he's out walking the trails not making a sound. All of a sudden he comes around a corner, and a bear steps onto the path. That's right, a bear. Now, Ranger Bob did at that time what we still recommend. He backed up slowly, and said, "Hey, bear, I'm going to let you have this trail."

Then he did something that we do not recommend, he climbed a tree. As soon as he got up in that tree, he looked down. That bear puts his little paws up on that tree. You guys ever see one of these spruce trees in the wind? The bear puts his back on the tree, starts scratching his back. [Laughter]. Well, pretty soon the bear walks back down that trail. Ranger Bob waited to make sure the bear was gone and starts climbing down that tree. But no sooner does Ranger Bob touch the ground when the bear comes back down the trail, only this time the bear has a friend. There are two bears coming down the trail. Ranger Bob climbs right back up that tree. He holds on with his arms and legs and sees one bear on one side, one bear on the other side. Now have you guys ever seen these spruce trees? Ranger Bob's doing this, holding on for dear life. [Laughter]. Oh, my goodness. The bears walk back down that trail. Ranger Bob learned his lesson. He stayed up in that tree longer this time. But no sooner than Ranger Bob touches the ground, what do you think is coming back around that curve? Three bears. This time, that first bear is there, but that bear has a beaver under his arm. [Laughter].

So I'm not sure if that's true or not, you know. [Laughter]. Some ranger legends might not be true. But that does help demonstrate some of the proper techniques of what to do with wildlife…

idea of how much those antlers weigh. And if I remember right my husband went up to try them. I didn't, but my husband did. So it was kind of cool.

The second emergent recollection was the general recall of the variety of animals the interpreter talked about in the program. As seen below, these memories certainly wouldn't be considered very specific, but nonetheless, were the responses gained two years after the program.

She talked about the caribou and the Dall sheep and the bears, which I thought was pretty neat there. I remember them talking about how animals survive. It's not as easy, animals got to hunt for food or look for food there and go through the extremes of the summer time when you get about a two month growing season and everything blooms and blossoms and produces fruit or what is seed all in a short period of time.

There is a life cycle that goes on and during that life cycle, as much as we like to see it all pleasant, there is some of this harsh reality. There is sickness and disease or something and sometimes there is especially hard winters or poor summers, lack of water, your animal populations will flourish with what food is available, what water is available in the park. You might have rise in population, decline in population, part of the natural life, life cycle.

YELLOWSTONE NATIONAL PARK/AUTHOR PHOTO

Hoosier National Forest Campfire Program
On a weekly basis, the Hoosier National Forest offers traditional campfire programs at a large amphitheater located in the middle of the agency's largest campground. This study focused on a program related to bats of Indiana. Approximately 50 visitors listened to an hour-long program that was to make visitors aware of the natural history of the bat and myths associated with bat behavior, and improve attitudes toward bats. The program started with a handout "test" that quizzed the participants on particular falsehoods regarding bats. Each of the questions was then answered throughout the evening. The statements included items such as, "True or false: Bats have the ability to suck blood from humans." The presentation included a 40-minute slide presentation along with a 15-minute question-and-answer period. The interpreter, a seasoned naturalist with over 20 years of experience, relied primarily on these two traditional program strategies. There were no hands-on items or other props.

Eighteen months following the campfire presentation, a sample of visitors was interviewed to learn what, if anything, they had learned or recollected about that program. Five themes relating to the participants' recollections were identified after the interview data was analyzed.

Novelty: From what the participants recalled, they tended to remember a part of the program that was novel or unusual, either in the setting or the topic presented.

> *I think because most of the time when you're getting information about animals maybe from the state park setting or whatever the setting might be, it tends to be indoors, and I think being outdoors, it is kind of unique and novel, and just, you know, a more enjoyable experience, because you can hear the sounds, the summer sounds, and that type of thing. So, it made it a little more memorable.*

In addition, some of those interviewed recalled the actual novelty of some of the bats they saw during the slide presentation.

> *They showed some really weird-looking bats. Some of them really, they weren't seen before, I guess. They're really weird, like the great big cute ears, or the face like a dog or something.*

Personal Significance: The participants recalled parts of the bat program when the information presented was important or relevant to them. These participants were all very concerned about their children's reactions to the program. They would notice and remember any part of the program that interested their children.

> *We had a bunch of kids…but even my seven-years-olds, they said pretty well they were interested [in the bat program]…I remember we talked about that [bat guano] and my kids thought that was really interesting. I thought they did*

inform us, and my kids did go home wanting to help bats…I think it is important for the little kids.

Why do I remember? I guess because we enjoyed this so much and the kids really liked it, and we liked it.

Speaker Qualities: Speaker qualities seemed to be another important factor that made the bat program more memorable for the participants in this study.

She was very good with the group as a whole. She took control of the group, because I know that being outside, you know, people had tendency to get up and do what they need to do, and kids are a little more apprehensive because it was at nighttime. She would just take control.

True/False Test: One type of "activity" appeared to facilitate the participants' recollection. The true/false "quiz" given prior to the program was recalled by some of the participants.

Food for Thought
With the exception of the true/false test at the beginning of the campfire, most of the Bats of Indiana program had a format that has endured over a century—a "lecture" from the naturalist, slides of bats, and opportunities for questions at the end. A traditional experience that offered some long term recollections and, to some, a different perception of this often maligned mammal.

They did give some sort of a true/false test. We handed it out, and we answered it, and we turned it back in. And they went over it whether they were true or false…. They kind of let us know, I guess, how people think they know that, but maybe realized that we didn't know as much as we thought.

I don't know. I liked that they did a little true/false thing…. We did probably learn more from that than anything because after we filled that out, we went over the questions. That was interesting to see which ones we got right, which ones we got wrong. So I think that was, that helped us learn more than anything.

Prior Knowledge/Misconceptions: Interviewees stated that the information presented in the program corrected the erroneous perceptions of bats they had held before the program.

I guess you always have an assumption. Your way of thinking of the bats is vampire bats and they're sucking animals' blood. And really I forget what percentage was or I don't think we have any in Indiana, and anything around like that.

I guess I remember most that we learned that [bats] are not blind—actually blind—and they don't suck your blood except for certain kinds…. They are good for the environment, for bugs.

The Denali National Park Dog Sled Program

If any program studied through this research would qualify as a large interpretive program, it would be the dog sled demonstration at Denali National Park. Each summer, over 50,000 visitors view the program, with an audience size that can range from 100 to 300 people, three times a day. The dog sled program is housed at a site that includes a historical museum, dog kennels, and a small arena for interpreter talks and dog sled demonstrations. During the program, participants had an opportunity to pet the dogs, visit the museum, talk with roaming rangers, and attend a 30-minute ranger discussion and demonstration about the historical and modern usage of the sled dogs in the park. During the formal program, the interpreter shared the rich history of the dogs and their use in the park, selected visitors to become a mock set of dogs (complete with sled attached), and led a dog sled pack around a small circle in front of the crowd.

Ten months following the 30-minute program, a sample of participants was contacted and interviewed to assess the impact of this historical, large-scale interpretive experience. Five themes emerged from their recollections: knowledge retention, the provocation of an emotional experience, a direct connection to the dogs and the program, a perceived change in attitude, and empathy towards the dogs and/or rangers that work with the dogs.

Knowledge Retention: Vivid knowledge retention was noted throughout a majority of the interviews. Participants primarily recalled information regarding the sled dogs, their use in patrolling the park, and the care of the animals.

> *They explained about using [the dogs] in the winter to patrol not only for skiers that come in, but poachers.*

> *I remember that they were using them since the park opened, I believe. It was the first way that they could get around. It is the best way they get around now during the winter time.*

> *...that the dogs were practically the first order of transportation and also that they drew the country together as far as their mail system went, etc.*

Other participants explained in greater detail specifics about the dogs. For example, below is a fairly detailed recall of the choice of a dog to perform the sled dog role:

> *Yeah, she talked about how it's not one type of dog. I mean, they look for traits of the dog, such as the feet, the fur, disposition, she also talked about you want to find dogs that can get along because you are going to be close with lots of human contact and then she went in to having the young pups tag along and while people bring dogs, walk them around, it's to keep the dog in training, move forward with them.*

Direct Connection: A sense of connection to the dogs and the program was a significant discussion topic among study participants, with general responses such as, "I enjoy working dogs," "I'm a dog person." The relationship with the animals was discussed by many of the participants.

Others commented more specifically upon their connection to the dogs as service animals and animal husbandry. One Alaska native discussed her connection to service animals, noting, "The dogs in Denali are what I would call a service dog. My husband now has a seeing-eye dog because he is blind." She later discussed her husband's service dog in greater detail, stating:

> *For 40-something years, he was very independent. He used a cane, he went wherever he wanted to go. We never thought of needing to have a dog until we planned on moving. And I have found she is such a cool thing to add to his life. She watches out for his safety and I think it's really cool how dogs can be trained to do a variety of services, and be dependable like that.*

Additional participants described unique, personal ways of how the dog sled program connected them to the park.

> *I got to know a little bit more about the history and about the dogs and how that whole program works and so we became more interested in the rest of the park and the rest of the stuff. I guess it was just sort of like an introduction, and it helped me become more interested in the park and learning about it.*

Emotional Experience: Emotions that were prompted by the dog sled program were found throughout the interview data amongst the participants. One participant stated, "I have to tell you how fascinated I was, how hard they wanted to work, how much they wanted to work in that extreme heat. It was just amazing." Another participant noted that within the experience,

> *You try to wrap your mind around what that means, but when you hear about a ranger and the dogs going out for two weeks and they get, I don't know, 100 miles and you realize that that's just a speck of the land. Yeah, it kind of gets you in touch with that notion of the specks we are on the planet.*

Other recollections described a sense of spiritual experiences, isolation and solitude, respect, and the need for stewardship. One participant suggested that the program made her feel like it was "a different world up there in the park. It's really nice, nice getaway, serene, God-like, you know, close to heaven." Another participant considered that:

> *After the dog sled presentation, I thought about the danger of it, and it's awfully cold and it's awfully isolated and the people who work there probably have some courage along with their passion for being there. And if you have to depend on somebody and you're way out in the boonies, I definitely would want to have a dozen or so dogs like that, somebody that I could depend on.*

Perceived Attitude Change: Perceived attitude change can be noted throughout some of the transcribed interviews. Participants often cited ways that their perceptions changed about the park because of the program and about the dogs being used for service.

> *I felt that these dogs were kind of pushed to do this and I think I came away with the idea that they really loved to do this. And they were so motivated to do it on their own that there wasn't any forcing to have them run and run and run. I think they convinced us that these dogs loved to pull sleds.*

Another participant's interview illustrated a similar perception of change of attitude, which may have stemmed from the program.

The dogs knew how they were treated. They would ruffle their fur and scratch them and talk to them, and the dogs, of course, when we first got there, we got there early enough to go around to see the individual dogs. At first I hated seeing them on a chain, but then I realized, well, they would probably have to do that. But they all seemed so happy and some jumped up on top of their little house, barking, carrying on. But you could tell the trainers really loved them and were taking good care of them.

Empathy: Some of the participants discussed feelings of empathy towards the dogs and/or rangers, which were derived from the program. Feelings regarding the rangers' occupations, respect for the dogs and rangers, as well as respect for the park and environment were present. One woman discussed how the experience really made her "stop to think of what it must have been like back then [when dogs were used for everyday travel], and what a phenomenal job these, these rangers have and how much you appreciate them and what they do and these dogs are just amazing." Another participant added that she gained "a deep respect for people who care for animals."

Food for Thought
Thirty minutes and a hundred plus other visitors watching—yet reactions, memories, attitudes toward the dog sledding and Denali were as personal and powerful as any program studied by the author.

Finally, the program's impact on one participant prompted the desire that, "It made us wanted to go to Alaska uh, forty years ago. And all it made us want to do is say, 'Oh, God, we should have gone in our younger days, we would have made our home there.' And we really lamented that we didn't." Later on in the interview, the gentleman noted, "Within the hour, I was talking to my sister-in-law about planning a trip for next year." He concluded the interview by stating, "It's something too bad every American doesn't get because it, it's an idea of how we have to maintain the purity of that area."

Yosemite National Park Tram Tour
Yosemite National Park is a site that is renowned for its beautiful views, geologic wonders, and human and natural history. A hallmark of the park's interpretive programs is the tram tour, allowing visitors amazing views of Yosemite Valley, as well as information about the geologic formation of the valley, its human history, and the wide variety of flora and fauna found in the area. During the program, visitors board a tram that takes them throughout the valley, providing views and information about the many waterfalls found in Yosemite and such well-known geologic formations as El Capitan and Half Dome. Visitors are exposed to the history of the National Park Service, park issues, animal and plant information, and current uses of the park, including rock climbing. The tram tour program is about two hours long and includes stops along the route for visitors to get off the

tram, take photos, and ask the ranger questions. During the program, the ranger sits in front with a microphone facing the audience while he or she provides dialogue concerning the things people see along the way.

This study represented not only a large group presentation (70 to 100 would be participating in the experience), but it also provided an extra challenge of accomplishing interpretive objectives while talking to the "passengers" in a 150-foot vehicle, all the while traveling 20 miles an hour. Six months following a tram program, participants were interviewed to learn of any lasting recollections. Three themes emerged from the interview data as key respondent recollections of the tour program.

Personal Connections: Several visitors mentioned connections that family members have with Yosemite. Some of these connections, as in the case of the first example below, were both personal and emotional.

> *I've been going to Yosemite for a great many years. My family and I would go there every Memorial Day weekend and then make reservations for the following year. It was our family together time. We'd never get tired of the park.*

Expanding upon family members' connections with Yosemite, other visitors mentioned personal connections they had with Yosemite. Some visitors remarked on connections they felt personally with the park.

He had talked a little bit about, which I actually remember from being a child, when they used to feed the bears there at the dump, and then they'd have the big firefall and you'd go watch the bears eat in the garbage pit. … Then as a child and even as an adult, we would camp there. My family used to camp there.

Ranger Attributes: In all studies conducted for this book, the impact and influence of the interpreter always came through in generally a positive light. (See Chapter 7.) However, the recollections from the tram tour were especially vivid and positive pertaining to "the ranger." These memories emerged spontaneously from visitor recollections and represented a variety of different subthemes.

Engaging Audience: Respondents recalled that the ranger was able to engage his or her audience through a variety of methods and techniques.

She engaged the whole tour. … It was engaging.

Everybody was pretty engaged. … He did really engage us.

It could have been really boring, but he did a really good job of keeping it interesting.

Knowledgeable and Experienced: An overwhelming majority of respondents described the rangers' knowledge and experience related to the park.

He had the answer that was by the book. … [He was] really knowledgeable in everything.

He did an excellent job of informing us about the things that were there. … He just knew everything about the place. … [He] kind of made you feel like he had spent his whole life there.

She would look out to the left or to the right and when it was time to start her commentary about what was coming up. … She could do it with her eyes closed.

General Positive Impression: An array of superlatives was offered by the participants during the interviews that gave a clear indication of the impact of the ranger on the tram tour.

She was a credit to the park service.

He did a really good job. … Whatever training he takes, they did a really good job. … We got off that tram and just went, "Wow, that was, he did an awesome job." … *We actually went over and told him that he did a good job.*

He told all those different little stories. … He told things in good, in little easy ways to remember, little stories. He connected you with whatever you were looking at, which for me helps me remember. … He had a good way of telling a story.

The Climbers. Since the last time the author had visited Yosemite was as a child, he, along with the tram participants, were surprised by the presence and influence of rock climbing. Throughout the tour, people were spending as much time searching for "climber sightings" as looking at the flora and fauna of the area. Hence, another prevalent theme from the long-term recollections related to the climbers.

We went by the climbing wall, where people were climbing, you could barely see them. That was really interesting.

I think they need to have some psychiatric help. … They sleep up there, so it was unbelievable. … I just can't imagine. … You know, there are people that try to do something a little bit over the edge.

I think they're stupid. … [There is] no way that I would put myself in a hammock on the side of a mountain and sleep over night.

Food for Thought
Not surprisingly—due to the mass mobile aspect of this interpretive experience—recollections were generally less rich than other studies conducted for this book. However, one message that wasn't lost by any of the participants interviewed was the impact of the interpreter leading the tram tour. One remark seems to reflect the impact of the interpreter on this particular large interpretive program: "Someone in our lives that does a good job and impacts our son in that way, we definitely go and tell them, hey, our son really enjoyed being able to do this with you. … In front of Bridal Veil Falls, [we] went and took a picture of my son and the ranger, the tour guide, together. … He lifted him up on top of this sign, and it was neat."

We couldn't imagine being out there and sleeping on the side of the mountains in a sleeping bag. … You can picture just rolling off. … You're just hanging there, and the wind and the elements are just full-force on you. … I couldn't do that.

He told about the guy that actually climbed that was a paraplegic in a wheelchair and would hoist with pulleys and the help of other climbers, he actually climbed.

Ironically, an iconic feature of the valley—its waterfalls—was soundly defeated in recollection by the climbers. Only a few comments were made during the interviews about the falls.

> *There wasn't much water. … Because of the time of year we went, so we really didn't see many of the falls. … My goal was to see water in the waterfalls.*

> *The only disappointment for us was that the falls were not falling. … By the time we got there, at that time of the year it was dry. I think maybe Bridal Veil had some water.*

The Bottom Line

Review of one of the oldest techniques of getting across an interpretive message—large group presentations—offers clear evidence that this strategy (through an array of formats) can deliver results. The five programs described and assessed in this chapter produced a variety of long-term recollections and even some attitude changes. The most successful techniques to draw out these memories seemed to be novel settings, subject matter, interpreter attributes, and active, hands-on opportunities. It is worth noting that the richness of responses to some of these programs equaled or exceeded much smaller-sized interpretive programs that are reviewed in other chapters. Hence, if properly applied, a person sitting with 100 other visitors may be able to get as much out of that experience as a person participating in an interpretive walk with 10.

4

Achieving Environmental Stewardship through Interpretation

Picture a room of 100 different interpreters from around the country. Then imagine a question being posed to them: "What is an ultimate goal of your interpretive program?" Since interpreters are artists in their own right, there will certainly be an array of answers. Goals could include historical or cultural awareness of a site, knowledge of recreational activities at a park, or specific information such as the flora and fauna of a site. In other words, there is a plethora of goals associated with the interpretive process. However, there is one area that a significant percentage of those 100 interpreters in the room will have in common—the desire to promote stewardship in their park or the site beyond its borders.

In 1997, the author completed an exhaustive literature review of all goals, principles, and objectives written by leaders in the interpretive profession. The sidebar on the next page is the result of the areas that were represented through the 101 outcomes found in this literature search.

As the results show, a sizable proportion of the leaders in the field (and, I would suggest, the 100 in the room) had a deep interest in promoting stewardship in and beyond the resource site they were interpreting. Current evidence also supports the idea of environmental stewardship and that it is still alive and well and a primary outcome for *many* interpretive programs.

Stewardship and Interpretation

Further evidence of the important relationship between interpretation and environmental stewardship is provided through historical context. The call for interpretive programs to lead to some type of action by the visitor dates back to the "father" of interpretation, Freeman Tilden. In his hallmark book, *Interpreting Our Heritage*, Tilden saw interpretation as a medium to promote a preservation ethic in the park visitor:

> Not the least of the fruits of adequate interpretation is the certainty that it leads directly toward the very preservation of the treasure itself. . . . Indeed, such a result may be the most important end of our interpretation, for what we cannot protect we are destined to lose. (Tilden, 1957, p. 37-38)

Soon after Tilden's work was completed, the National Park Service embraced the idea of interpretation as being a conduit for stewardship. For example, in December 1967, Bill Everhart, assistant director for interpretation for the National Park Service, declared:

101 Outcomes of Literature Review

Category	Citations
Environmental Stewardship	22
Appreciation of Site	9
Understanding of Site	8
Awareness of Site Policies	8
Information	8
Environmental Awareness	7
Enjoyment	7
Awareness of Site	4
Stimulate / Inspire	4
Visitor Orientation	4
Fulfill Management Goals	3
Recreation	2
Visitor Feedback	2
Environmental Education	2
Miscellaneous	11
	101

> We have not effectively carried out an educational campaign to further the general cause of conservation. . . . Only through an environmental approach to interpretation can an organization like ours . . . achieve its purpose of making the park visitor's experience fully significant. (Mackintosh, 1986, p. 67)

The beginnings of environmental interpretation were clearly evident when Earth Day 1970 swept the country into an environmental consciousness. A solidification of the term environmental interpretation came through the National Recreation and Parks Association's publication, *Islands of Hope*. It was this text that defined and attempted to validate the use of environmental interpretation to promote "environmental reform" (Brown, 1971).

For the next three and a half decades, a significant portion of the leaders in the interpretive field have continued to call on its professionals in parks, zoos, nature centers, and resource agencies to inform constituents about the natural resource site and urge them to influence and change their visitors' behavior toward the use of the natural resources being interpreted. For example, the most widely used textbook in interpretation during the 1980s, Grant Sharpe's *Interpreting the Environment,* places the action/behavior goal as one of the three superordinate objectives of interpretation:

> Interpretation can encourage thoughtful use of the recreation resource on the part of the visitor, helping reinforce the idea that parks are special places requiring special behavior . . . interpretation can be used to minimize human impact on the resource in a variety of ways. (Sharpe, 1982, p. 4)

There is no evidence that this support for action as an outcome of interpretation diminished through the years. In fact, during the early 1990s there seemed to be a resurgence in the desire to see the field make dramatic effects on the resource site visitor. Dr. Roderick Nash, keynote speaker at the 1991 NAI National Workshop, reflected this future optimism:

> Interpreters have a challenge to help visitors realize the highest potential of a park or reserve. . . . The development of an environmental ethic might be thought of as the culmination of this process. It will be one of the most important frontiers of interpretation in the 21st century. (Nash, 1991)

But certainly the most descriptive outcome goal for interpretive programs during the early 1990s comes from the National Park Service's Goals for Interpretive and Educational programs. The first goal states:

> Promote the parks as learning laboratories to develop greater public awareness, understanding, appreciation and commitment to the preservation and/or restoration of the National Park System and the larger environment on which they depend. From local neighborhoods to the global community, move people from awareness to action. By interpreting local resources and issues assist the public to see how they fit into the larger global community and move them from awareness to action on resource protection and management issues. (National Parks Education Task Force, 1990)

Today, the call for environmental stewardship through interpretation continues to be a fundamental mission for many of the leading organizations associated with interpretation.

Stewardship through Interpretation

The interest in promoting environmental stewardship through interpretation motivated the author to develop a model for attempting to achieve such an important goal. This work was based largely on two sources—literature related

The Relationship Between Environmental Interpretation and Environmental Education

There is a close relationship between environmental education and environmental interpretation. Both fields have a great deal in common as suggested by a variety of leaders in each profession. They certainly share terminal goals—to produce individuals that can make responsible environmental decisions. Despite the similarities, interpreters and environmental educators must grasp the differences in order to develop successful partnerships.

Although the ultimate aim of environmental interpretation and environmental education may be similar, the inherent nature of both fields creates two clear contrasts. First, the structure and characteristics of both professions are different. Environmental education tends to be associated with formal institutions that require students to participate in a sequential learning process. Interpretation, on the other hand, tends to be voluntary and located in recreational settings. Most interpretive experiences, at best, cover a period of two hours to half a day. As Gail Vander Stoep explains, "Typically [interpretation] occurs in settings that are informal or nonformal; target audiences are voluntary; the interpretive experience is usually short term (single, standalone experiences) rather than part of a series over an extended period" (1995, p. 470). On the other hand, curriculum development in environmental education is based on the premise that a student becomes invested in environmental issues (Hungerford & Volk, 1990). This variable is predicated on a period of time longer than the average interpretive experience can offer.

The lack of time with constituents creates a significant gap in attaining the behavior change goal associated with both environmental interpretation and environmental education. Several research studies regarding environmental behavior list important variables associated with this desired change. Two of the most crucial variables are an individual's in-depth knowledge of environmental issues along with an investment of time regarding these issues. *People need time to attain the sensitivity, knowledge, and attitudes necessary for a positive environmental ethic. Time is certainly one characteristic that an interpretive experience lacks.*

The second important contrast with environmental education is interpretation's lack of credible program development goals associated with behavior change. For the past 25 years, the field of environmental education has been guided by a set of established principles. These guideposts (the Tbilisi Doctrine) were produced at an international environmental conference in 1977 and consisted of a series of hierarchical learning objectives. The Tbilisi Principles have been the foundation for the development of several theoretical models in environmental education. These directives have laid the groundwork for research and development in theoretical and action-based models that have produced several reputable environmental curricula. Environmental interpretation, on the other hand, is based on six principles written by one man (Freeman Tilden) 50 years ago. Although his principles are important directives, the field has not developed a "road map" to achieve some of his attitudinal and behavior change goals.

to environmental interpretation and curriculum development in environmental education. The latter was utilized due to the close linkage between both for the past 40 years. Of particular value were the Goals for Curriculum Development in Environmental Education developed by Hungerford, Peyton, and Wilke in 1990. The Goals for Curriculum Development in Environmental Education were hierarchical in nature and culminated in responsible citizen behavior in an environmental dimension. They have also withstood the test of time and have been used as the framework for many of the leading environmental education programs throughout the country.

The synthesis of interpretive literature (such as principles, goals, and objectives from leading interpretive sources) with the goals of environmental education resulted in the development of the Goals for Program Development in Environmental Interpretation which is outlined below:

Goals for Program Development in Environmental Interpretation

Level I: Entry-Level Goals
Component A: This level seeks to provide the visitor with sufficient resource site information to permit him/her to be knowledgeable about aspects of the resource site.
Component B: This level seeks to provide the visitor with experiences that promote an understanding or comprehension of resource site information.
Component C: This level seeks to provide the visitor with sufficient knowledge to permit him/her to become aware of the resource management policies and goals of the resource site.
Component D: This level seeks to provide the visitor with experiences that promote an empathetic perspective toward the resource site.

Level II: Ownership Goals
Component A: This level seeks to develop a cognitive awareness of how visitors and their collective actions may influence the quality of the natural resource site. It further seeks to develop an awareness of how these same individuals may influence the quality of other environments.
Component B: This level provides for the knowledge necessary to permit visitors to investigate and evaluate natural resource site issues.

Level III: Empowerment Goals
This level seeks to develop skills necessary for visitors to take positive and responsible environmental actions in regards to resource site issues.

Environmental Interpretation Behavior Change Model
The model on the next page further illustrates the relationship of all three goal levels. The most powerful use of the model is to offer interpretive experiences that

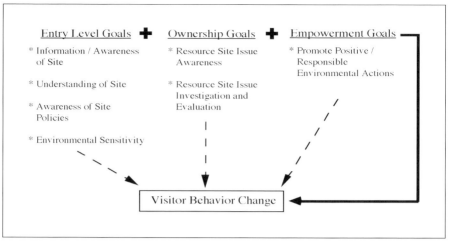

Environmental Interpretation Behavior Change Model

represent all three goal levels in a sequential hierarchical order. Although this may not assure attitude or behavior change in the visitor, it does offer opportunities to stimulate this change. It is important to note that with the exception of issue investigation goals, all of the directives listed in the above model are outcomes often found in the interpretive literature.

Testing the Model
Research was conducted to evaluate the impact of each of the three goal levels on potential knowledge, attitude, and behavior intent of the visitor. The populations for these studies were students (grades 3 through 7) from various school districts in southern and northern Indiana. Although not considered representative of the general public, schools do make up a great proportion of the interpretive audience. Each of these studies used a quasi-experimental design to approximate conditions of a true experiment in a setting that does not allow for control of all variables (Isaac & Michael, 1990). Students in each of the studies completed pre- and post-questionnaires. A statistical analysis was performed to evaluate significant impact of the interpretive experience on knowledge, attitude, and/or behavior intent toward the resource site.

Study 1: Impact of Entry-Level Goals
The first study (Drake & Knapp, 1994) represented an interpretive experience that engaged in entry-level goals—ecological awareness, awareness of the site policies, and environmental sensitivity related to the site. This study evaluated 300 third- and fourth-grade students prior to and following a half-day visit to a community garden and nature center. Through a series of meetings with participating school

Goals for Curriculum Development in Environmental Education

The superordinate goal is to aid people in becoming environmentally knowledgeable and, above all, skilled and dedicated people who are willing to work, individually and collectively, toward achieving and/or maintaining a dynamic equilibrium between quality of life and quality of the environment.

Goal Level I: The Ecological Foundations Level
This level seeks to provide learners with sufficient ecological knowledge to permit him/her to eventually make ecologically sound decisions with respect to environmental issues.

Goal Level II: The Conceptual Awareness Level—Issues and Values
This level seeks to guide the development of a conceptual awareness of how individual and collective actions may influence the relationship between quality of life and the quality of the environment and, also, how these actions result in environmental issues which must be resolved through investigation, evaluation, values clarification, decision making, and finally, citizenship action.

Goal Level III: The Investigation and Evaluation Level
This level provides for the development of the knowledge and skills necessary to permit learners to investigate environmental issues and evaluate alternative solutions for solving these issues. Similarly, values are clarified with respect to these issues and alternative solutions.

Goal Level IV: Action Skills Level—Training and Application
This level seeks to guide the development of those skills necessary for learners to take positive environmental action for the purpose of achieving and/or maintaining a dynamic equilibrium between quality of life and the quality of the environment. (Hungerford, Peyton, & Wilke, 1980, p. 44)

teachers and agency officials, an interpretive program was developed that answered the needs of the teachers' class curricula. The actual experiences and activities used in these programs were taken from existing environmental and conservation resources such as Project Learning Tree, Project Wild, and OBIS (Outdoor Biological Instructional Strategies). The subject matter contained in the interpretive experience focused on plant adaptations. This was an important science concept that both the third- and fourth-grade students were learning through the Science Curriculum Improvement Study (SCIS). These interpretive programs lasted for a half day and were led by an environmental education specialist.

The results of this quantitative study showed significant changes in students' knowledge of plant adaptations after their interpretive experience. All knowledge questions associated with the pre-post instrument showed significant gains following the nature center program. However, questions related to attitude changes did not show significant changes following the interpretive experience.

Study 2: Impact of Entry Level Goals and Ownership Goals
A second study (Knapp & Barrie, 1999) compared an interpretive experience that offered entry-level goals (ecological awareness and site policies) with an interpretive program that represented an aspect of ownership level goals (resource site issue awareness). Approximately 1,600 fourth- and fifth-grade students participated in these field trips at the Indiana Dunes National Lakeshore. A half-day interpretive program was offered once in the fall and once in the spring. Both

field trips were designed to be conducted in an outdoor setting and experiential in method. The only difference between the two field trips was the content of the interpretive program. The fall session covered basic ecological concepts (a Level 1 goal) while the spring concentrated on environmental issues relative to the park (a Level 2 goal). They both took place at the Paul H. Douglas Environmental Education Center located on the western boundary of the national lakeshore.

The fall ecology program included student participation in investigating differences among habitats encountered on a guided walk. The "Habitats Hike" enforced the theme that the variety of habitats at Indiana Dunes National Lakeshore support an abundance of animal and plant life while each of these habitats contains a mixture of different conditions under which certain plants and animals can survive. The spring program was based on environmental issues associated with the national lakeshore. The program "A Grain of Truth" was designed to introduce the theme of why humans impact the dunes and help participants realize the influence humans have on the succession process of a dune ecosystem. A variety of other environmental issues were conveyed to the students during the interpretive hike.

The results supported the notion that both an ecological and issue-oriented interpretive experience can impact knowledge. Following each program, students showed significant gains in knowledge about the dunes ecosystem (fall program) and issues related to the dunes (spring program). There was, however, no significant impact with regards to change in affect or behavior following either program. Participants in both the issue-oriented and ecological field trip showed no increase in affect toward the site, nor did environmental behavior increase following these experiences.

Study 3: Impact of Entry-Level, Ownership, and Empowerment Goals
A third study (Knapp & Marsan, 1996) evaluated the impacts of an interpretive partnership that represented each of the three visitor behavior change goal levels—entry-level, ownership, and empowerment. Approximately 30 seventh-grade students participated in four interpretive experiences along with a research assignment supervised by the participating classroom teacher. In an attempt to provide an educational experience that promoted the full range of goals associated with the behavior change model, a partnership was formed between the United States Forest Service and the local school corporation. These institutions pooled resources to offer a one-year pilot study that combined environmental interpretation with a middle school's science curriculum.

Unlike traditional "one-shot" interpretive events, the Forest Service provided four interpretive experiences that represented a sequential environmental education curriculum. These experiences included:

Basic Knowledge of a Wilderness Site
    This first field trip focused on basic ecological principles regarding south

central Indiana ecosystems, as well as the natural and cultural history of Indiana's only designated wilderness area.

Awareness of Problems and Issues Associated with Wilderness Site
Students learned about the problems and issues associated with the wilderness by analyzing some wilderness site issues and examining certain wilderness problems.

Investigation of Wilderness Site Issues
Strategies and methods were taught with respect to collecting data and summarizing results. Students developed surveys and performed class research projects during this period.

Knowledge of Citizen Participation Skills
Students were taught methods of communicating their results in a public setting. In addition, students were taught different action skills related to responsible environmental behavior.

Wilderness Summit
The final aspect of the interpretive/school partnership was a meeting with the U.S. Forest Service officials to report recommendations regarding management of the wilderness. These recommendations were

a result of their surveys and research completed during the final phases of the program.

The quantitative results indicated a positive change in students' knowledge of the wilderness. There were significant increases in the students' understanding of both the ecology and issues associated with the wilderness area. However, despite the depth and breadth of this program, quantitative analysis showed no increase in attitude or change of behavior in students toward the wilderness or related issues. These results counter qualitative observations conducted by the author. But ultimately, quantitative evaluation found no significant findings related to behavior.

The Bottom Line
These three studies offered interpretive experiences that involved objectives representative of all of the goal levels in the behavior change model. The studies showed that all goal levels promoted significant gains in students' knowledge regarding the basic awareness of the resource site. Information such as plant and

Pandora's Box

It seems simple enough—offer an interpretive program that shares the environmental degradations that humans have caused. Pro-active behavior is the only logical product from such enlightenment. Certainly hundreds of programs across the country attempt this task in one form or another. However, some of the research conducted has found an opposite effect. In particular, with children, the author has found that as students learned more about environmental issues—for example, stresses on wilderness sites—the more some of them became "fatigued" by the complexity and shades of gray within environmental issues. Results from the wilderness project (Study 3) showed that the students seemed to think that they were not capable of making a significant difference. A number of students responding to questions such as, "Do you plan on taking action?" answered with "Not really" or "No….I don't think I'd do a big thing to help support it because it seems like there is a lot more resistance to keep it open than to shut it down." A lack of locus of control seemed more pervasive during the post questioning. As one student remarked, "I am just 12 and I can't do anything."

Programs such as the wilderness interpretation project can crack open a "Pandora's Box" that contains a glimpse of the complexity and multidimensional aspects of environmental issues. Due to their brevity, interpretive experiences cannot allow proper time or rumination for students to understand and assimilate complicated issues. So what is the solution? Keep the box closed unless you're prepared to have it fully opened. In this case, be prepared to offer a holistic view of the issues—which would necessitate more time than many interpretive experiences can offer.

animal adaptations, forest ecosystems, wilderness issues, and dune ecology were retained. However, there was no significant data that showed that any of these programs impacted the students' attitude or behavior intent toward the resource site or beyond. For example, participants in Study 1 did not change their attitude regarding their interest in learning about plants, nor did they increase their interest in learning about nature as a whole. Students in Study 2 showed no increase in positive attitude regarding the park they were visiting or about wanting to participate in an interpretive program in the future. Similar findings resulted from analysis of Study 3's participants. Attitude about visiting a wilderness after their interpretive experience at such a site did not improve. The results of Study 3 also showed that students' intent to ask others to support environmental actions or individual letter writing did not increase.

Each of the three studies reviewed above offered interpretive experiences that fulfilled the objectives included in one or more of the major levels of the Program Development Goals for Environmental Interpretation. Unfortunately, results of

A View From The Back Row

In a middle school auditorium in southern Indiana the Hoosier National Forest Supervisor calmly outlined the future of the access policies to the Charles C. Deam Wilderness. A gravel road that bisects the 13,000 acre wilderness would remain open... Before this statement the atmosphere in the assembly was similar to many other middle school events. A handful of students were attentive while the remainder seemed disinterested. However, as the speaker voiced the decision to keep the road open, a different mood enveloped the room. Many students began asking more specific questions about the issues. The candid replies from the Forest Service brought even more hands into the air. The prior apathy was replaced with a relentless pursuit of answers to a variety of important questions. Eventually, the moderator offered the closing comments and the students resumed their normal schedules. An assembly that was scheduled for forty-five minutes lasted nearly an hour and a half due to a strong interest in a wilderness the students knew nothing about one year earlier.

The apparent interest of these middle school students was the product of a year-long interpretive project that established a unique partnership between a local school district and community environmental education resources. The emotional yet thoughtful questions posed to the Forest Service officials reflected an investment made by these students regarding a local environmental issue. Through an intensive five-phase program it was hoped that these students would take ownership in a variety of problems and issues in a federal wilderness area located in the southern portion of their county. And certainly from the author's view from the back of the auditorium—the ownership was alive and well.

these three studies offered significant impacts only at awareness or understanding levels. These findings would suggest that the most success for an interpretive program (at least school students) to affect goals related to actual environmental stewardship is difficult to attain. However, further research through qualitative means has uncovered a bit more success in other goal levels for both school students and adults.

Tried and Proven Techniques toward Stewardship

The three studies described in the previous section represented six years of quantitative analysis of interpretive programs. Although this work represented tens of thousands of dollars of research money and intensive work in data analysis, many questions remained as to interpretation's actual impact on stewardship—the ultimate goal of the model discussed above. Therefore, the author began to change research strategies toward qualitative measures to attain richer results that could learn more about individuals' impact toward stewardship following an interpretive experience. The following section offers results from some of these qualitative approaches that give more clarity to long-term impacts of environmental interpretive experiences. Comments made by children and adults recorded by the author and research associates suggest a range of impacts from interpretive programs long after they were presented.

Ecological Awareness
> *And then there is a clog like in a pipe that goes up to the surface. And when it heats the water and gets really, really hot, it puts a bunch of pressure on it and it eventually lets it, all the pressure go.*

> *The pine cones of the trees in extreme heat open up and get buried in the ash and they grow and it starts the forest all over again.*

> *I learned that steam is visible, water vapor is not.*

> *Underground geysers are like plumbing systems. They start at the area where the water is and gets heated up by the earth's core.*

> *That the wolves almost became extinct in Yellowstone and ones were reintroduced and people were saying that the wolf would ruin the ecosystem, but they didn't, they really helped them out because all the sick animals were taken by the wolves, which made the herds stronger.*

These recollections of ecological facts pertained to the Yellowstone National Park *one year* after the students' visit. This was part of the subject matter that was offered during *Expedition: Yellowstone!*—a one-week residential environmental education program offered in Lamar Valley. During the week at *Expedition:*

Yellowstone!, students experienced a variety of environmental education activities, hikes, and lab investigations. Subjects included geology, water ecology, forest management, and Native American history. The week-long program based much of its educational strategies on hands-on, interactive experiences.

Environmental Attitudes

> *I guess if I see a bat, I am not as scared as I probably would have been or I feel more comfortable for my kids to see a bat…. [Bats] are not dangerous, and not to be scared of them.*

> *Before the program, I didn't really like them. I thought they carried rabies and they would bite, I just figured that [bats] are not gonna be too dangerous or anything." Just because so many people have such a misconception about [bats]…. Maybe especially the kids understand that they are not dangerous, they are not gonna attack us, you know, [bats] are not a bad mammal, they just have bad reputation.*

These remarks were recorded a *year and a half* following a one-hour evening presentation on bats of Indiana. The location of the program was a campground amphitheater in the Hoosier National Forest. The general objectives of the presentation were to make visitors aware of the natural history of the bat, make visitors aware of the misinformation about negative bat behavior, and improve visitors' attitudes toward bats.

The program included a 40-minute slide presentation along with a 15-minute question-and-answer period. The interpreter, a seasoned naturalist with over 20 years of experience, relied primarily on these two traditional program strategies.

Environmental Behavior

> *It impressed my husband to the point where he's like, "Okay, from now on, when we go back, we're going to be taking public transportation." … We can get trains as far as Modesto. … We'll take a bus from there, but we're not going to use our own car next time. … The next day, we went and joined the Yosemite Association because of the tour.*

> *[The tour] left an impression in me that we need to do something about tourism in the park. … We took the inner-park shuttle bus, which is natural gas powered.*

> *Some of those things that I've thought about a lot are the influx of people and things like that. And you know, why there's limited parking. … Until we do, we need to just take it easy.*

These comments came from visitors *eight months* after their participation in Yosemite National Park's valley tram tour. During the two-hour ride, visitors were exposed to the history of the National Park Service, park issues, animal and plant information, and current uses of the park. During the program, the ranger sat in front with a microphone, facing the audience while he or she provided dialogue and underlying information concerning the things people saw along the way.

The three programs described above, along with long-term recollections of these programs, offer some hope that interpretive and non-formal environmental education experiences can illicit outcomes associated with levels of the environmental behavior change model described previously. Specific environmental knowledge was certainly gained through the Yellowstone experience. Attitudes towards bats seemed to be influenced even a year after participating in a campground program. And it seems that, at least for some, behavior toward Yosemite National Park was altered following their tram ride program.

Are these results the norm? Unfortunately, not. In the many research studies this author has conducted there is little evidence stewardship is attained—in the long term—following an interpretive event. Certainly knowledge has been gained and in some cases, even attitudes may have been affected. But evidence that visitor stewardship toward the resource or beyond has been limited at best. This should not be such a surprise since attempting to change an individual's behavior—which promoting stewardship represents—is a difficult task, especially when it is approached in a format that is usually less than an hour.

Despite this daunting challenge, it is *exactly* what the field asks its professionals to accomplish. As noted at the outset of this chapter, there is a rich history for wanting to promote stewardship and, in some cases, change the world.

Here are some examples of this expectation:

> Interpretation must not only fulfill the aspirations of conservationists but also should act as a major force for the social, economic, political, and cultural good. Interpretation should encourage and motivate individuals and groups to participate in decisions concerning alternative futures and appeal to people at an affective as well as a cognitive level. (Ballantyne & Uzzell, 1993)

> According to tradition, [interpretation's] goal is not simply to teach audiences factual material about the environment but, rather, to impact their point of view, and sometimes behavior, with respect to managed resources or protected values. (Ham & Krumpfe, 1996)

Agencies and institutions associated with the profession still place a great deal of importance in attaining stewardship through interpretive experiences. For example, a core value of the National Association for Interpretation is to "connect people with their cultural and natural heritage to promote stewardship of resources" (National Association for Interpretation, 2007). The National Park Service's Interpretive Development Program is designed to accomplish several goals, including "a higher level of public stewardship for park resources." (National Park Service, 2007)

Successful Strategies for Environmental Interpretation
So how does interpretation come to terms with this disconnect? The answers are not simple, but certainly one strategy would be to understand its strengths in relation to influencing stewardship and focus on those directions during the precious time an interpreter has with his or her constituents. Here are some suggested strategies that may help and that seem consistent with the research:

Focus on the Entry-Level Variables
The notion of emphasizing the basics is not a new concept. Certainly, the roots of interpretation are grounded in the call of John Muir: "I'll interpret the rocks, learn the language of flood, storm, and the avalanche. I'll acquaint myself with the glaciers and wild gardens, and get as near the heart of the world as I can" (Mackintosh, 1986, p.6). The research outlined above reinforces this initial mission of the profession, which casts doubt on the effectiveness of interpretation beyond its original intent of revealing information. In fact, this basic objective may truly be the most important outcome of interpretation. Today, there is a growing sentiment to return to the basics and to offer—children, in particular—conduits for contact with the outdoors. Richard Louv has become a prominent spokesperson for this lack of connection with the outdoors. In his instant classic, *Last Child in the Woods: Saving Our Children from Nature-Deficit Disorder*, he states:

Experiences that *Do* Promote Lifelong Stewardship

So what *does* promote environmental stewardship? There certainly has been no lack of studies attempting to answer that question. However, the answers are often derived from short-term investigations that offer variables that certainly may be important, but are not actually "tested" through a time span that would truly reflect lifelong value and behavior changes (the author has his share of these types of products). The closest look at influences on lifestyle changes comes from a series of studies based on significant life experiences. The notion and rationale for investigating significant life experiences comes from an explanation by the founding expert in this area, Dr. Thomas Tanner:

> A venerable premise of the environmental education community is that the education of youth should produce adults committed to environmental quality, adults whose behaviors consistently evidence that commitment in their life roles. There is a growing body of studies which aim to identify formative influences in the lives of persons who more or less approximate that ideal. The rationale for such research is simple: if we find that certain kinds of experiences that were important in shaping such adults, perhaps, environmental educators [and interpreters] can replicate those experiences. (1998, p. 365)

Hence, several researchers, including Tanner, interviewed adults who demonstrated pro-environmental tendencies, individuals who had careers or lifelong patterns of promoting and practicing stewardship. All of the research related to similar life experiences of those individuals:

- positive experiences in natural areas
- adult role models
- environmental organizations
- education
- negative experiences (first-hand) of environmental degradation.

In particular, experiences with peers or adults in the outdoors, at an early age, for a long period of time, seems to be one of the more influential variables. This took the form of repeated camping trips with families, spending childhood time in outdoor pursuits such as hunting, fishing, and formal camping programs.

Are these surprising results? In answering this question, take the time to recall how you acquired your interest in the outdoors and its stewardship. Chances are it was gained in a similar fashion. But more importantly, for the sake of this book, ask this question: Did I become a steward of the environment because of a field trip to a park, or because of a ranger-led program, or a talk with an interpreter? If your answer is no, then more than likely you are among the majority who gained their environmental "ethics" through a longer, more substantial approach—such as childhood / family experiences.

In the space of a century, the American experience of nature has gone from direct utilitarianism to romantic attachment to electronic detachment…the one that young people are growing up in today. And there is a growing body of evidence and expert opinion that "electronic detachment" is deleterious to physical and mental health, resulting in "nature-deficit disorder." (2006)

Connect the Environmental Message to the Visitor
If one finding from this book becomes apparent, it would be the success an interpretive message has when it connects with the visitor's own life. This tenet doesn't change in approaching environmental messages. In several of the author's research studies, there were individuals whose interviews following their interpretive experience reflected a much deeper sensitivity to the environmental concepts or subject matter they had retained. A consistent trait of these individuals was their specific connection to the topic. For example, a woman who participated in the dog sled program at Denali had more of an interest and inclination toward stewardship of the area due, in part, to the direct relevance with her family:

> *My mother was born and raised among glaciers, so I'm kind of familiar with some of the use of those dogs, then—snowmobiles and stuff. The program was sort of like positive reinforcement of things that I have heard my mother talk about. My mother grew up out there when it was still pretty much wilderness.*

Another visitor to the Yosemite tram tour offered much more recollection and interest in the program than others. Her connection to the park and hence interest in the topic became quite evident:

> *I remember talking about my mom and how when she was 11 they traveled in, like, a Model A from Oakland down to Yosemite. And she had fallen asleep, she was a kid, between a couple of big, hot grown-ups in the middle of the summer in a car. And going to Yosemite with no air-conditioning, of course. And she woke up at Valley View and cried because she thought she was dead. Then she looked around and cried harder because she thought they were all dead and everybody had gone to heaven. … I always think of Valley View because I know it was my mom's favorite.*

Clearly the advantage these two visitors had over other participants was their previous connections with the resource site. However, more often than not, every audience has one or more of these types of folks who has personal connection(s) to the program's topic. Hence, it would seem fitting to spend a bit of time during the program learning who may have past connections and "exploit" them for the good of the connection.

An extension to optimizing personal connections is an approach to "IMBY"

(In My Backyard) the interpretive message. For example, a program on wildlife at any resource site offers a range of potential. But through all the visuals and dialogue that can accompany such a topic, nothing could be more enriching to the visitor than offering challenges to the audience to find similar flora and/or fauna in their own backyards.

Handle Environmental Issues with Care
Although the origins of interpretation were simply to reveal information and wonders of nature, there became a growing interest to have interpreters do more to make visitors aware of the resource and the environmental issues associated with these places. As the issues regarding our environment grew during the 1960s and 1970s, the call for interpretation to be a change agent continued to grow. Today, the desire to impact a visitor's behavior toward the park is paramount. Unfortunately, this call for interpretation to solve the environmental ills of our society is not reflective of the actual impacts that this medium can attain. And as noted previously, some research shows a negative reaction to some types of issue awareness.

The "Pandora's Box" effect has been a concern with others in the field. Michael Weilbacher brought this issue to the profession over a decade ago when he stated, "Eight-year-olds should not be asked to become warriors or worriers. Children have much more important work to do: Watch ants. Grow flowers. Dance between raindrops" (1994, p. 28). David Sobel eloquently explained this concern through *Beyond Ecophobia: Reclaiming the Heart in Nature Education*. In it he warns educators of ecophobia:

> A fear of ecological problems and the natural world. Fear of oil spills, rainforest destruction, whale hunting, acid rain, the ozone hole, and Lyme disease. Fear of just being outside. If we prematurely ask children to deal with problems beyond their understanding and control, prematurely recruit them to solve the mammoth problems of an adult world, then I think we cut them off from the possible sources of their strength…. What's important is that children have an opportunity to bond with the natural world, to learn to love it, before being asked to heal its wounds" (p. 9)

This certainly is not suggesting we ignore issues—we cannot and must not. But they should be offered sparingly and with great care when it comes to younger audiences. And most certainly, they should be presented to adult audiences with the utmost non-biased, factual precision. For example, as we move through the next few decades, global climate change issues will be apparent and paramount at many resource sites. Hence, rather than avoid them, we should interpret them with the utmost scientific backing and not through personal speculation.

Be Pragmatic

Our profession has an excellent body of research that *does* support the notion that it *can* impact basic awareness of a resource site. It does *not* have the same evidence that it can move beyond this aspiration—nor does it need to. We can only *hope* to create stewards of our environment through a chance visit with an interpreter. We can only *wish* that a visit to a park will motivate a person to act responsibly toward that site. We can, however, *reveal* to them the beauty of the resource and the power of nature. We can also make them aware of the intricacies of this environment. These basic, yet crucial, goals are ones that interpreters *can* accomplish. They can form the foundation for the attainment of our ultimate goal—environmental stewardship.

5 One-on-One Interpretation

A Magical Moment

It was the most special night I had shared with my daughter. Although I wish I could say it was through spending an evening camping in a secluded forest, the truth of the matter is that this evening occurred in the middle of Americana— Disney World. What's worse, the experience was in a mock outdoor setting called Fort Wilderness with a visit to watch Chip and Dale's Campfire—a classic Disney experience. The 1,000-seat amphitheater was spotless and overseen by a staff that was totally service oriented—another Disney trait. However, all of this "perfection" that comes with a visit to Disney was not the cause of our once-in-a-lifetime experience. Instead, it began with one of the staff coming to my daughter (a.k.a. Maddie) and beginning a conversation that quickly escalated to an invitation for her and me to go "back stage" to meet Chip and Dale, get autographs, *and* be a part of the campfire program. If there is such a thing as instant nirvana, my five-year-old had achieved it. With the professionalism and organization that Disney is known for, we were quickly led to Chip and Dale with the opportunity for my daughter to engage in "conversation" (of course, chipmunks don't talk) and loving hugs. Then, we were given an autographed photograph of the rodents in their natural habitat (adjacent to Cinderella's castle).

We were then led like royalty to the front row of the amphitheater, where I sat down while the staff led Maddie to the stage to be a part of folk songs that were led by Chip, Dale, an entertainer, and my daughter. At the end of this surreal experience, the staff gave Maddie a certificate that stated:

> *This moment was certifiably magical.*
> *Across the miles and over the years,*
> *You'll always remember this magical moment*
> *From Walt Disney World.*

We were one of one million individuals chosen during the year to have a "Magical Moment." And there still isn't a week that goes by that we don't reference to that evening for one reason or another. As time passed, I realized that my daughter and I were a part of a Disney scheme that was genius. There is no doubt that a trip to Disney is memorable, but to be singled out with the attention given to my daughter and me made the trip something beyond compare. If we weren't hooked as a Disney family before our trip, we certainly are now.

One-on-One Interpretation

So what does this family recollection have to do with interpretation? Actually the parallels are not hard to comprehend. Consider a family that takes a week-long trip to Yellowstone National Park (or some other resource site). During their visit, they have a direct encounter with a park interpreter who offers the family a viewing of a "secret spot" or the awarding of a ranger badge to a son or daughter after taking a special park pledge—a personal experience that certainly could turn an ordinary park visit into a potential long-term memory.

The realities of our profession would seem to deflate the notion of one-on-one interpretation. In particular, lack of staff, time, and money to offer such experiences would seem sufficient to squelch such an approach. But there are scenarios that would suggest that this type of face-to-face interpretation would be just what a resource site could use to offer the most "bang for the buck" of an interpreter. Below are two scenarios observed by the author that would support such an approach:

How Far to the Top?

The highest point of the Great Smoky Mountains National Park is Clingman's Dome, a high-visitation site that sees tens of thousands of people walking a steep, half-mile, paved trail to reach the summit and observatory. Following the conclusion of an observation of a school field trip, I accompanied a ranger down the steep path to the parking lot. During the short jaunt, Ranger Mike was stopped at least five times to answer the question, "How much farther till we get to the top?" Although the question required a brief response, Ranger Mike had the ability and skills to offer much more information to these folks, including why all

the trees looked dead and why the viewshed wasn't clearer. Several of the people who stopped Ranger Mike had atypical garb from the normal "demographics" that an interpretive program would represent. One had a Jeff Gordon NASCAR shirt, another a Harley Davidson tattoo, and a third was sharing a pack of cigarettes with his friends. Call it a hunch, but these were people who would probably not be signing up for the wildflower walk offered later that day down at the visitor center. Here was a case of one-on-one interpretation to people who would have had no intention to partake in an interpretive experience, but yet they got one right between the eyes. Was it a "Disney moment"? Probably not, but it was a chance for those people to realize the park had approachable and knowledgeable staff, while learning some important natural resource information.

Pardon the Interruption
Located at the southern end of Yellowstone National Park is the Grant Village district that includes the West Thumb Geyser Basin. On one particular fall day, the researcher was tagging along with an interpreter as she led her participants on a 30-minute walk along the boundary of the geysers. The seasonal staff member had only been able to lure five people on her walk, which was a classic "drag and brag" approach to an interpretive hike. Nothing seemed out of the ordinary with this program, with one exception. During the 30-minute walk, she was interrupted by other hikers querying about location of restrooms, best viewings of the geysers, etc. In other words, since her original group was so small, many thought she

wasn't engaged in a program, but rather, walking with a large family. The point to this vignette is the economy of time and money. The interpreter would have had to have time to prepare for the guided hike, attempt to market the event, and then offer the program that may or may not have made a connection with the audience. On the other hand, if she would have just taken a slow walk around the trail she would have reached *more* visitors with *relevant* information—a face-to-face approach based on the visitors' terms and not the interpreter's.

The Art of Roving

These scenarios suggest a strategy that has been well documented in the interpretive field: roving. It is an interpretive technique that can (and should) take place in virtually every area of a resource site. This could include a visitor center, overlook, campground, trail, or any other place where visitors will be found.

- *Roving* interpretation is personalized, face-to-face communication where the audience has chosen the venue, the resource is the stage, and the interpreter is the catalyst for knowledge.

- *Roving* provides the means to protect the resource and the visitor and to ensure a quality recreational experience.

- *Roving* interpretation may seem spontaneous, extemporaneous, impromptu, unstructured, ad-lib, or unprepared, but this is not the case. When done properly, it is well organized and planned.

The cruel reality of the interpretive profession is that less than 20 percent of visitors actually participate in a formal program. Therefore, the need to be proactive and take the park's message to the visitor is crucial. Roving is one way to meet that objective. There are important variables associated with successful roving. Below are four common sense tips that should be heeded when practicing roving.

Location, Location, Location
The examples shared above show the importance of the location of the interpreter in increasing the odds of quality face-to-face time. This may not mean that the roving take place at the busiest site of a park (i.e. in front of a visitor center) but rather a place where people are most likely at their "terminal" destination of an experience. In many cases, these locations will enhance the odds of a question from a visitor and, with any luck and skill, the interpreter can create his or her own program with a gathering audience.

Timing is Everything
Although the notion of roving would suggest an unstructured day, the actual implementation of the technique should be carefully choreographed with

optimum times of visitor contact. However, since the strength of roving is its "teachable moments," the interpreter should always be ready to stop and chat with a visitor, even if he or she is on the way to lunch.

Having a "Hook"

Wearing a park uniform may be enough of a draw for visitors to be attracted to a roving interpreter. However, it may not hurt to have some type of prop or "hook" that can help reel in an audience. For example, following the author's observations at Haleakala, the staff began to institute a roving "program" where they periodically set up an odd-looking solar panel. Like bees to honey, visitors began to drift to the ranger to learn of the strange contraption—and so the program on Haleakala and the cultural history of the sun gods begins.

A Balancing Act

One of the greatest deterrents to roving is the difficulty of the approach. Unlike a program that has a beginning, an end, and a safe space between the interpreter and audience, the idea of face-to-face communication with the public is daunting. And in many cases, the only way to get comfortable and "good" at it is through experience—in particular, reading the folks on the other side of the conversation.

Props Versus Programs

During a fall afternoon in Great Smoky Mountains National Park, a table was set up in front of the Cades Cove Visitor Center. It held a variety of historical artifacts from the Appalachia era circa the early 1800s. Among the items were toys of the era, which were particularly being scrutinized by children, who, in turn, drew the adults closer to the table. A very personable park volunteer supervised the items and was offering tidbits of information—excellent one-on-one interpretation complete with hands-on props. After an hour of displaying the props and answering questions from many visitors, the interpreter closed up to prepare and conduct a formal program tour of the historic area adjacent to the visitor center. Though the program was listed in the *Smokies Newsletter*, advertised at the visitor center, and announced through a posted sign at the head of the trail, *two* people participated in the walk.

The irony of this scenario is obvious. One hour of artifacts on a table attracted tens if not hundreds of one-on-one moments, while a well-prepared and well-marketed walk resulted in a personal tour for a couple from the neighboring state of Kentucky. While the table of touchables is common in nature centers, it is less frequent out in the resource (i.e. along a trail or near a historic building). However, the success described above has not been lost by many resource sites—in particular zoos and aquaria—that are using organized one-on-one approaches more often and decreasing their schedule of formal programs.

Be sensitive to cues that suggest they have had enough one-on-one engagement. Certainly, if your dialogue is "short and sweet," they actually may begin to ask more questions to keep their conversation with you going.

Unlike other interpretive strategies, roving is difficult to assess. Few research studies have been conducted in this area due to its spontaneous structure. In this book, studies have included impacts on school field trips, day hikes, visitor center programs, museum tours, boat and tram excursions, campfires, and star observations. Audiences are defined and then contacted and the areas of retention are apparent. In the case of roving, spontaneity makes such tasks virtually impossible to complete. Therefore, this chapter relies on observations of roving experiences that *did* occur and scenarios where it was not used but *should* have been.

Tried and Proven Roving Encounters

Yosemite Valley Tram Tour
A premier interpretive experience at Yosemite National Park is the valley tram tour. During the two-hour ride around the boundary of the valley, the tram takes a rest stop at an overlook, where participants can use public facilities and take pictures. On one of these tours, the interpreter was especially outgoing with the visitors and made it a point to "mingle" and, in essence, practice some roving interpretation. Recollections of his personal appeal and apparent interest in visitor needs came through 10 months after the program:

> We really liked the guide. He really did a good job and was very knowledgeable. You know, there wasn't a question he couldn't answer. We went in front of Bridal Veil Falls and took a picture of my son with the ranger…it was neat! We have talked about [the interpreter] and the connection he had with my son…. We were at first going, "Wow it's kind of expensive to take the tour." But afterwards we both said it was well worth the money.

> He said something about, "I should know about a perfect dome." And took off his hat. He was, like, totally bald. … That was hysterical. After six months, that's what I remember.

> He was sort of waiting for the people that were on the tour to sort of bring up some questions, and he would launch into answers about those. I honestly think the fact that he sort of left the floor open for questions was a very good idea, so he could run with that. I talked to him at one of the stops when we stopped by the river. … Then I talked to him after the tour just for a second or two to say I enjoyed it and thanks a lot and I asked him some other question.

> I don't know if the age had something to do with that, because I would imagine we're fairly close in age. … A lot of his interests were probably similar to mine.

RANGER TAKING PHOTO OF TOURISTS DURING REST STOP AT YOSEMITE TRAM TOUR/AUTHOR PHOTO

After we got off at certain spots, you'd go up to him and he was very willing to talk to you.

Denali Dog Sled Demonstration

The dog sled program is housed at a site that includes a historical museum, dog kennels, and a small arena for interpreter talks and dog sled demonstrations. Prior to the organized program, interpreters and dog trainers are available for visitors to come up face to face (with both dogs and staff) and learn about the care and maintenance of the dogs. In other words, scheduled "roving" takes place prior to the actual demonstrations. Recollections of these close encounters eight months after their visits proved to be fruitful and potentially attitude changing.

We got the impression that all of those people who worked with the dogs had waited quite some time in order to be selected to get over there so they could work with the dogs.

Oh, I thought the relationship between the dogs and the caregivers and the rangers was just phenomenal. It was just like, there was so much love and so much trust and so much caring because as soon as they, after they had hooked them up to the sled and the dogs went around that small circle and ended up back in front of us, um that the caregivers were right there with bowls of water.

They [dogs] are so excited, I mean the thing is they're friendly to anybody, you can go up and pet them, you know and everything was so clean, so neat and you could just see these dogs were happy.

Well, I thought it was wonderful, they had the dogs sitting there by their little kennels and you could talk to them and you could pet them, you know, it was, uh, it was very nice and, you know, the fact that they were working dogs.

They were handled very well. Yes, they were. They weren't mistreated or anything. They were handled very well.

The two vignettes give a glimpse of the impact that direct contact with interpreters, staff, and dogs can have on visitors long after the experience. None of these memories was formed from a formal program, but rather, from close encounters on a one-to-one basis.

The Ones that Got Away

As noted previously, assessing the impact of roving has not been a primary focus of the research related to this book. Hence, actual documented impacts are limited to the two studies above. However, this researcher has observed a variety of programs for other assessment purposes and has concluded that there were many times that one on one techniques would have been fruitful, but were not utilized.

The Good, Bad, and the Silverswords

As part of a research commitment to Haleakala National Park (located on the Hawaiian Islands), one of the assessment tasks was to observe the summit area to gather information on visitor patterns. The summit of the volcano is the primary stopping point for the park and receives the most visitation of any area on the mountain. A tale of two interpretive approaches emerged from my work—a good one and a bad one.

The bad news first: One of the staples of interpretation of Haleakala is to offer a talk in an observatory that is located on a corner of the summit. The staff was frustrated with the lack of visitors actually attending these scheduled programs. So one of my tasks was to learn why there was a paucity in participants. Observations of the interpreters' on-site "marketing" of the program uncovered an influential reason for the lack of attendance. Fifteen minutes prior to the presentation, the ranger (who would have to drive from the visitor center to the summit parking lot) would get out of her car and walk directly to the observatory and wait diligently in the overlook for participants. Meanwhile, the summit area itself would typically have 50 to a 100 people at any given time exploring the area and the many spectacular views. In other words, the interpreter assumed people would come to her (hidden in the observatory) while, in reality, they were exploring the summit ridge, taking in sights at their own pace. Hence, the ranger would manage to catch a handful of listeners while the majority was roaming on their own.

Now the good news—sort of: One of the aspects of this park that differentiates it from many others is the variety of privately run tour guides—quasi-interpreters who operate small businesses that take vacationers to the volcano. One such operation—a bit on the rustic side, at best—had the answer to the park's observatory visitation dilemma. This man's strategy was to let off his van load of clients and then walk to the iconic plant species of the park, the Silversword plant. Wearing a camouflage jacket and jeans and smoking a cigarette, he immediately began to approach people and ask if they knew anything about the plant they were looking at. Within minutes, his burly voice and animated style attracted 20 to 30 people to the plant where he proceeded to give a "program" on the plant and the history of its use—all the while passing out his business card to drum up more paying customers for his all-day excursions.

This scenario is not to suggest that park staff change their uniforms and begin to smoke. But it does highlight the potential success of aggressive, one-on-one interpretation that can turn into an all-out program. It also points out an important factor to successful "roving." The individual must *want* to talk with people and, in fact, seek them out. Unfortunately, many interpreters observed through our research studies were quite content to plan a program, go to the program site, and then give the program. Any disruptions from this pattern would just be considered an inconvenience.

Below are examples of direct encounters that were simply missed.

A Tale of Two Owls

On a chilly fall day, a group of visitors was arriving at an amphitheater to listen to a bird of prey demonstration. Fifteen minutes prior to the program, 30 people were seated and the interpreter was ready for her presentation. The birds, a barred owl and screech owl, were securely placed on the stage along with a variety of raptor catch-and-release equipment. The visitors were visibly intrigued by the "props" and the interpreter was visibly uncomfortable with the "free time." So, she sat up on the stage and waited—and waited—until 2:00 p.m., when the "interpretive experience" could begin. Fifteen precious minutes of discourse between families and a park representative were lost. As our research has noted, brief one-on-ones with the programmer and the visitor can carry a great deal of weight. It would not be a stretch to suggest that if she had engaged with the early birds she would have had participants that may have had a memorable up-close moment and a group of people feeling more invested in her program.

Prep, Preach, and Pull Out

At a scheduled evening program on wildlife, an interpreter had a whopping five visitors in an auditorium that could hold up to 100. Instead of facing the obvious, this programmer plowed ahead with a 40-minute slide presentation, all the while lecturing as if there were a full house. This included the classic approach of giving no opportunity for questions until the end of her oration. This type of inflexibility is, unfortunately, a common occurrence. As this chapter has noted, the comfort level of professionals to step out of the "prep, preach, and pull out mode" is difficult. This interpreter had a golden opportunity to "converse" with five visitors—one on one—and learn what they were about, where they had come from, and what they wanted to know—information that she could have used to make connections that would prove to be much more meaningful than the diatribe she inflicted on the handful in the room.

The Quiet Voyage

In Chapter 2, the Lowell National Historical Park canal boat program is reviewed and offers strong support for personal connections made during the tour that translated to rich recollections of the experience and the themes desired by the park staff. Hence, there was clear success to these programs and the visitors seemed pleased with both the interpreters and the program. However, there were opportunities lost evident in the departure of each group from the boat. As people left, there was a lack of "chatter" between participants and the programmer. In other words, after being in a small canal boat for almost an hour and experiencing a variety of novel and historic experiences, little exchange had taken place between passengers and the interpreter. One reason for the lack of rapport was the lack of one-on-one moments. In the rare cases that the interpreter was not pointing out a site or lecturing on a historical topic, there was silence—dead silence. It was the type of uncomfortable void when a group is clumped into an elevator and the piped-in music stops. These dead zones were perfect opportunities for the interpreter to actually ask questions to the participants, such as, "Does anyone here know of a friend or family member who worked in a mill?" As the research has noted there were plenty of memories and stories that could have been shared by the passengers. Often, someone sitting near me would whisper a story about a relative or a friend who worked in a mill like the one we were passing. This was personal information that could have been a part of the interpretive dialogue— recollections that could have further enriched the trip and bonded the passengers.

The Bottom Line

Successful roving may be the most difficult technique to master. It may be the most uncomfortable of all of the approaches for an interpreter to carry out. It also is one of the hardest experiences to actually evaluate. However, it may well be the most important strategy of the future. Today, the use and viability of personal service-oriented interpretation is challenged by inexpensive signage and other passive techniques. The increase in face-to-face, one-on-one, ranger-to-visitor encounters may be just the medicine needed to improve the health, viability, and significance of personal interpretation.

6

The School Field Trip

The school field trip has been a staple of interpretation since the profession's early days of Enos Mills and the Trail School. It is an important aspect of nature centers, parks, zoos, aquaria, cultural sites, and other places where interpretation is practiced. In many places, the school field trip is the sure customer when public programs wane in attendance as the summer months draw to an end. Today, there are thousands of schools across the country conducting field trips to interpretive facilities to aid in achieving curriculum goals and objectives.

Along with the rich and important history of the school field trip comes the fact that these informal education experiences do make a difference. A variety of research related to field trip programs have data that show strong support for the notion that they can and do promote cognitive learning. There is also evidence that field trips create a positive impact on attitudes related to the program site and the subject matter. In short, school field trips are important aspects of both interpretation and formal education.

The Basics of a Field Trip

Key Components
As with any educational approach, the field trip has key components that need to be in place to ensure success. Below are three important variables that can give meaningful structure to the field trip experience:

1. The main instructional strategy of the field trip should be hands-on experiences concentrating on activities that cannot be done in the classroom.

2. A process-oriented approach should be used to achieve field trip objectives. This approach would include strategies such as observing, touching, identifying, measuring, and comparing.

3. Students should be prepared for the field trip. The more familiar they are with the subject matter of the experience, the more productive the trip will be for the students.

Stages of Field Trip Development
Field trip development can take place through the completion of the following four stages:

Stage 1: Hierarchical Organization of Curriculum Concepts:
    The curriculum associated with the field trip is classified according to its concreteness or abstraction level and assigned appropriate teaching environments, whether it is in the classroom or at the field trip site.

Stage 2: Educational Mapping of the Field Trip Site:
    This stage includes a review of which areas of the site may serve as study stations. The objective of this review should include a clear notion of the educational outcomes that would be accomplished at each area. Factors in choosing these stations should include variables such as spatial requirements for students, safety, and, of course, pertinence to the content being conveyed.

Stage 3: Planning The Field Trip Program:
    This stage involves the actual organization of the study stations to answer the objectives or goals of the curriculum concepts. Some of the points that should be addressed during the planning of the site program would include the actual time involved in moving groups from one station to the next and the time involved at each station.

Stage 4: Development of Teaching Materials and Learning Aids:
    In order to answer the goals or objectives of the curriculum associated with

the field trip, a variety of items would need to be produced or be available. This would include audio-visual aids, equipment for field activities, and lab sheets, if needed.

An Educational Process for the Field Trip: The Learning Cycle
A popular and proven educational strategy to convey field trip content is through the Learning Cycle. Based on educational theory developed by Jean Piaget, this educational approach incorporates five stages: Engagement, Exploration, Explanation, Extension, and Evaluation.

Engagement:
    In this initial stage, the interpreter attempts to create interest and generate curiosity in the topic of study as well as raise questions and elicit responses from students that will give the interpreter an idea of what his or her audience already knows.

Learning Cycle Diagram

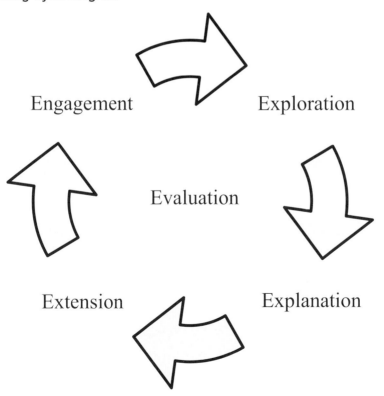

Engagement   Exploration

Evaluation

Extension   Explanation

Exploration:

> During this stage students should be given opportunities to work together without direct instruction from the interpreter, who acts more as a facilitator. This is a chance for students to explore, observe, and hypothesize particular situations or sites. Questions and observations that should be openly discussed will arise from this exploration.

Explanation:

> At this stage, the interpreter provides definitions and explanations for the questions and observations that arise in the Exploration stage.

Extension:

> This is an opportunity for students to apply concepts learned from the explanation phase. This can take place at the same study station or, ideally, in a different area. Exploration strategies apply here because students should be using the previous information to ask questions and make new observations.

Evaluation:

> Evaluation should take place throughout the learning experience. Interpreters should observe students' knowledge and/or skills, application of new concepts, and changes in thinking. Students should also have the ability to assess their own learning.

Keeping the Field Trip in the Classroom

Although it is sometimes difficult to accomplish, the field trip and its associated topics should directly relate to the curriculum offered back at the classroom. A great deal of evidence points to much more retention of content when it is offered to the students prior to and after the experience. In order to integrate the field trip into the school curriculum, three primary steps or units would need to be accomplished:

The Preparatory Unit:

> This unit is based on concrete learning activities that would take place in the classroom one to two weeks prior to the on-site program. These lessons would be chosen by the classroom teacher with the aid of the interpretive site staff.

The Field Trip:

> The on-site program would offer both concrete and abstract ideas that are more difficult to convey in the classroom. Interpreters leading these experiences would attempt to link the on-site content with subject matter discussed previously in the classroom.

A Constructivist Approach

As with other aspects of interpretation, a field trip can be enhanced through a constructivist approach. A major theme in the constructivist framework is that learning is an active process in which learners (in this case, the students) construct new ideas or concepts based upon their current or past knowledge. The interpreter and the students could engage in an active dialogue (i.e., Socratic learning), with the interpreter presenting information that matches with the students' current state of understanding.

In essence, the interpreter could *include* his or her audience in the program as much as possible. Below is a "conversation" an interpreter had with her participants as they hiked to the top of Loft Mountain during a field trip in Shenandoah National Park:

> *Good to see you folks up here. My name is Ranger Kathy and I will be leading you up the mountain and talking with you about the rocks in the area. So, Amber, as we go along do you think we'll see a lot of rocks along the way?*
>
> *I would say, "Yes?"*
>
> *Well, I think you're right. We should see a lot of different rocks. Jesse—do you have any idea what kind of rocks might be up there on the top of the mountain?*
>
> *Big ones!*
>
> *Well sure, but I guess I was wondering if you thought they would be metamorphic, igneous, or sedimentary. Let me try you folks this way—which of those types of rocks have you been studying in school?*
>
> *Igneous! Metamorphic!*
>
> *Great. Let's keep an eye out for these type of rocks as we go up the mountain.*

This was only the beginning of a back-and-forth communication that Ranger Kathy had with her trail group during the field trip—a constructive conversation.

The Summary Unit:

This step would be completed back in the classroom and would attempt to tie together the concrete and abstract information conveyed in the preparatory and field trip units. Summative assignments such as essays would give students a chance to synthesize information gained from the previous units.

A Tale of Two Field Trips

To illustrate the impact of classroom preparation prior to and after a field trip, a summary of the recollections of two very different field trips is depicted below:

A fifth-grade class in Indiana took a field trip to a city park that includes a large forest and a nature preserve. The three-hour field trip included a guided hike and several activities related to environmental science.

There was *no* classroom preparation and *no* follow-up regarding the trip.

One year later, students were contacted to learn what they remembered regarding the trip. Every student who was interviewed offered little to no recollection of the content that was offered during the program. In fact, many of these students hardly remembered what they even *did* at the park. Below are two examples of interview responses:

I remember we learned about nature

I think we learned about plants and played a game.

Avoid the "Novelty Factor"

It is a Catch-22 of the interpretive field. The "class site" for the field trip is usually an exciting or novel place, such as a beautiful forest, a significant historical site, or a particular park. They are places significantly more "exciting" than the four walls of a classroom. While these special sites offer intrigue to both the interpreter and the student, they also offer a novel setting that many times overshadows the educational message that is conveyed at the site. Research has shown that the more classroom preparation that occurs prior to the field trip, the less the students are awed by the scenery and the more accepting they are of the field trip's message.

Another fifth-grade class in Virginia took a field trip to a nearby national park. The program content for this field trip was geology of the area.

Unlike the first class, these students completed two weeks of pre-field trip activities and wrote an essay following the trip.

One year after the program, the students were interviewed to learn what they remembered regarding the trip. Both content and activities were vividly recalled. Below are two examples of interview responses:

We were studying rocks in science at school and they wanted us to take a field trip up here to help us with that and we had to take a test on rocks and I think that probably helped me a good bit, on remembering what, like rocks and all.

Before I went, I thought a rock was just a rock, but when I got there I learned about the different types and the rocks, um, how they come from lava to certain rocks and how it all goes back to lava again…like the rock cycle.

Field trips that are a part of the class curriculum are more effective.

Tried and Proven Field Trip Techniques

A Little Talk and a Lot of Touching Go a Long Way
In a variety of settings, with a range of school students, particular hands-on activities have had the ability to stay with students long after the field trip. But more importantly, these activities have enabled students to *learn* concepts.

Activity: Bag of Rocks
Location: Shenandoah National Park
Audience: Fifth-Grade Students
Educational Goal: Become Aware of and Identify Basic Geologic Formations

Scenario: During the course of a hike to the top of Loft Mountain in Shenandoah National Park an interpreter stops the students in her trail group and takes out a bag that contains rocks. The first challenge is for the students to feel the rocks while blindfolded and note differences in texture and form, etc. Following this task, the rocks are then placed in piles according to their outward characteristics. At this point, the interpreter discusses each pile and distinguishes them as igneous, sedimentary, and metamorphic.

Results: This activity took approximately 30 minutes out of a total of a four-hour field trip. Although brief, this experience was critical in aiding students' retention of geologic formations. *One year* after the field trip, one student said the following about the activity:

They divided us into groups with, like, maybe three or four people in each group and they gave us each a rock and a little bit to look at it to figure out what it was. We discussed it as a group and then at the end, everybody had to stand up and say what they thought it was. And she, she'd explain it and tell us whether we were right or wrong and why each rock was what it was and, like, how old it was and, like, how it was formed.

More importantly, when asked what the educational message of this activity was, students had responses like this one:

Well, one of the rocks was igneous, which are formed from just-cooled lava, and another was sedimentary rock from, like, sand and stuff that gets built over time and hardens together and then another rock was metamorphic rocks—those have just gone through some kind of change.

Certainly, for this field trip, a bag of rocks went a long way.

Activity: Under the Hat Scavenger Hunt
Location: Hoosier National Forest
Audience: Fourth-Grade Students
Educational Goal: Become Aware of Aspects of Nature's Food Cycles

Scenario: During a three-hour field trip to Hoosier National Forest, students from a local school district participated in several different experiences to help them learn about a range of environmental topics. One of these activities was a scavenger hunt in which the interpreter placed natural items under his ranger hat. These items represented aspects of the food chain and food web. He then lifted the hat for 10 to 15 seconds so students could memorize the objects and find similar items in the forest. Following the students' collection, the ranger summarized the objects that were under the hat and how they related to food chains.

Results: Six months after the field trip, students were asked what they remembered and/or learned regarding their visit to Hoosier National Forest. One of the more vivid recollections was of this scavenger hunt:

> He had a hat on a board and each group lifted up the hat—and we had 15 seconds—to look at what was underneath. There was a berry, a piece of wood, and other stuff, and then he put the hat down and you had to find them.

> It taught me more about how the systems work, like the food chain and what kind of plants are in nature.

Although the responses were more general in nature than the bag of rocks activity, the scavenger hunt was found to have the ability to help students retain some conceptual knowledge. The differences in the results and the way the two activities were delivered seemed to make a difference. The interpreter with the rocks offered much more discussion following the activity than the interpreter with the hat.

Activity: The Cup, The Straw, and The Woolly Adelgid
Location: Great Smoky Mountains National Park
Audience: Fifth-Grade Students
Educational Goal: Make Students Aware of the Impact of Woolly Adelgids on
        Fraser Firs

Scenario: One of the more popular field trips to Great Smoky Mountains National Park is a hike up to the top of Clingman's Dome—highest peak in the park. Along the way, national park interpreters offer a variety of educational activities to convey topics such as high-altitude ecosystems, air-quality issues, and invasive species impact. One 20-minute activity that is conducted during the hike includes a paper cup, straw, and tacks. In "Partners," one student is a woolly adelgid (thumb tacks) and the other student is a Fraser fir attempting to suck up water from its roots (cup and straw). As the adelgid increases the number of times it sticks holes in the tree (the straw), the harder it is to bring up water. This process exemplified the impact the adelgid has on the Fraser fir and hence the destruction of this species in the park.

Food For Thought
Despite the brevity of each of these activities in relation to the field trip, they each packed a punch for long-term retention and knowledge gained. It seems clear with these examples that when you have hands touching content (both in the physical and cognitive sense) the message will linger long after the bus has left the park.

Results: No other activity or experience related to this field trip carried as much weight as did this experience with a cup and straw. Retention of the activity, and especially its message, was as vivid as any field trip technique analyzed for this book. Here are two representative responses from students *one year* after the program:

> *And the one who had the cup and the straw would start drinking a little bit of water, and then the partner with the tack would poke a hole in it and this was all about the bugs that were attacking the trees and the trees were dying because they couldn't get water from the ground.*

And if that wasn't specific enough:

> *Some of us were like this woolly delphid [actual name woolly adelgid] and some of us were trees and so the trees got their straws and the woolly delphids got thumbtacks…so the tree people couldn't suck as good, and then we poked a whole bunch of holes in the straw and it didn't work at all. So anyways, they talked about what the woolly delphid was really doing.*

This is an interpreter's dream come true. Over a year after the interpretive experience, children still understood that there is a nasty little bug (woolly adelgid) that is killing all of the Fraser Firs. All because of a Dixie cup, straw, water, and a thumb tack.

Games, Games, and More Games
As most interpreters know, games and field trips go together like bees and honey. It is a rare field trip during which the interpreter does not offer a game for either educational purposes or just to get the energy out of his or her "squirrelly" students. It may come as a surprise, however, the impact these games have on students' recollections of the field trip and the educational messages that are retained from playing the game are significant.

Game: Migration Headache
Location: Hilltop Garden and Nature Center (Bloomington, Indiana)
Audience: Third-Grade Students
Educational Goal: Make Students Aware of the Challenges Birds Face When They Migrate

Scenario: A field trip to the Hilltop Garden and Nature Center usually focuses on topics related to horticulture since the facility is a small (five acre) organic garden. However, this particular field trip investigated different types of animals that might live in and around gardens. During the two hour program, students participated in Migration Headache. This game is well known by Project Wild users and has been played in settings throughout the country. The game has students run from one end of a field to the other pretending they are migrating birds. The students attempt to stop at resting points that periodically get taken away to symbolize ecological and environmental challenges that may occur.

Results: Students that participated in this field trip were interviewed *three years* after the program. First, it must be noted that there are inherent challenges in any long-term research, but it is especially difficult when it entails such a long time and the subjects are sixth-graders who attempt to recall something that occurred when they were third-graders. Therefore, it was not surprising that recall of the program was either very general or nonexistent, with the exception of one experience, the Migration Headache game. Most of the students who were interviewed could describe the game in this typical manner:

I remember that we had to run and jump on circles so that we wouldn't die.

Interviewer: *Do you remember what the circles were for?*

INTERPRETER LEADING A GAME AT HILLTOP GARDEN AND NATURE CENTER

We were birds and we were trying to get food while we were migrating

Interviewer: *Do you remember why you did the game?*

Yeah, it was so we knew that flying and migrating is hard.

This answer may not seem significant unless it is put in the context that these students remembered a game three years after they played it *and* kept the primary message of the experience—migration is a headache.

Game: Predator/Prey
Location: Hoosier National Forest
Audience: Fourth-Grade Students
Educational Goal: Make Students Aware of Predator/Prey Relationships Indicative
    of Southern Indiana Ecosystems

This game was the concluding activity of a four-hour field trip to Hoosier National Forest. The game's structure, popular with teachers and interpreters alike, has been called different names with different educational goals in mind. This rendition had students break into two groups facing each other. The interpreter would call out an animal's name to one group, which they would then represent, and then call out a different animal for the other group to represent. If one group had an animal that was the prey of the other group's animal, they attempted to flee before the predators ate (tagged) them. Several predator/prey combinations were called out with group sizes fluctuating with each feeding cycle. Finally, the last relationship was called out: "Okay, one group is bull frogs and the other group is bull frogs. Total chaos ensued, with students bumping into each other and laughing hysterically. Once the chatter died down the interpreter explained that bull frogs are cannibalistic.

Results: Six months after the field trip, almost all students who were interviewed vividly recalled the predator/prey game and, in particular, learned that frogs are cannibalistic:

We played stuff like "Predator and Prey." And one group would be the predator and he would tell them two animals and you had to figure out which one would be the predator and which one would be the prey. And then the predator would chase the prey.

One side was this certain animal and the other side was a certain animal. It was like a predator game. If you were like a predator you tried to get the other students. And the last one he called was frogs because they were cannibalistic.

The recollection of the game and the cannibalistic frogs was one of the most recalled aspects of this field trip. Certainly, students no longer saw bull frogs in the same way, thanks to this game.

Game: Camouflage
Location: Yellowstone National Park
Audience: Sixth-Grade Class
Educational Goal: Make Students Aware of the Adaptations of Animals in the
    Yellowstone Ecosystem

Scenario: One of the larger educational programs at Yellowstone National Park is *Expedition: Yellowstone!* This is a residential environmental education center that schools from across the country visit to learn about the greater Yellowstone ecosystem. Unlike the other field trips discussed in this chapter, this experience is a residential one that has students stay approximately five days in the beautiful Lamar Valley. Although a different and lengthier field trip, the results are consistent with findings from a three-hour field trip at a neighborhood park.

Camouflage was played during an all-day hike on the last full day of the residential program. The game, similar to the two described above, is a popular activity that is used by both teachers and interpreters. It is similar to hide-and-seek in that one student closes his or her eyes and the rest of the participating students find a place to camouflage, making sure they show at least a part of their body during the game. The student who is "it" attempts to find as many students

STUDENTS PREPARE FOR CAMOUFLAGE GAME YELLOWSTONE NATIONAL PARK/AUTHOR PHOTO

as possible without moving. Two to three rounds are played to enable those students who are not found to come closer and camouflage themselves. It is a very simple game with obvious linkages to ecological concepts such as predation and camouflage.

Results: The *Expedition: Yellowstone!* program offers five days of dramatic scenery, first-class educational programs, and a variety of hands-on labs in some of the most pristine environments in the United States. Therefore, it wasn't surprising that one year following the experience, students still had elaborate accounts of their week. What was surprising was that some of the most vivid accounts and descriptions were saved for the camouflage game:

> *There was one person that was "it" and they had to stand in the front of a field of sagebrush, then turn around and count to 20 and everyone had to go hide, and then he would turn around and pick out all the people, he could see, and when he couldn't see any more people he would turn his back and count to five and everyone would run to a new place that was closer.*

Interviewer: *So what was the point to the game?*

How animals camouflage.

Food For Thought

Many interpreters consider field trips as an important opportunity for students to learn as much as they can about the site they are visiting. Therefore games are viewed by many as a necessary evil. However, their impact, both emotionally and cognitively, has been found to be quite dramatic. In particular, the more embedded the content is with the game itself, such as the cannibalistic frogs in the predator/prey game—the higher the chances that both the enjoyment and the learning are retained.

Not only was the game a memorable experience, it was a highlight of the week to many of the students:

> *It was fun to dive to the ground, and was fun because our teacher even tried it.*

> *It was my favorite part of the trip because it was informative while you had fun playing a game that you know how to do.*

> *It was just a break from what we were doing. It was a challenge, but fun in that it made you think how you could get around bushes without anyone seeing you.*

In summary, one of the highlights of a five-day residential program in Yellowstone National Park was a game that could have been played in any field or forest throughout the country.

The Novelty Factor
One variable that seemed to be in almost all field trip research was considered the novelty factor, an experience or sighting that may not have been planned or considered as novel, but one that certainly carried weight with the children.

Experience: All-Day Hike
Location: Yellowstone National Park
Audience: Sixth-Grade Class
Educational Goal: Make Students Aware of the Variety of Habitats and Ecosystems in the Park

Scenario: One of the days of the *Expedition: Yellowstone!* (discussed previously) is an all-day hike that has students trek five miles though some of the classic meadows and forests of northern Yellowstone National Park. After only 30 minutes into the hike, the interpreter stopped the students and turned to the audience, looking a little ashen, as if he had seen a ghost. Around the turn was a full-sized male bison lying right in the middle of the path. Those who have visited the park in recent years have learned that the most dangerous animal encounters have not been with grizzly bears but with bison. So, understandably, the interpreter took this encounter very seriously, which the students picked up on quickly. He adjusted their hiking route to traverse a steep hillside to avoid the large beast.
    Results: One year later, the students clearly remembered the encounter and

STUDENTS TRAVERSE HILLSIDE TO AVOID BISON YELLOWSTONE NATIONAL PARK/AUTHOR PHOTO

brought it up periodically during the interviews. Certainly, this encounter was not planned, but its novelty—and a sense of danger—made it a lasting impression.

> *And we were hiking and there was one right in the middle of the path where we were going. And then we had to go about 100 yards away up in the trees so we avoided it.*

> *[The ranger] was up front, and we just, we were walking single file and we stopped and started looking around and he finally said, it's a, it's a bull moo, it's a bison, that is. We need to get up and around him so he doesn't charge or anything. So we went up a side hill and walked and he finally stood up, and we got down and he turned the other way.*

Food For Thought

The first experience at Yellowstone discussed in this chapter was certainly not planned, while the second one is a permanent fixture of the site. The examples suggest that parks may have opportunities that can be created or enhanced that can give the students a "Whoa!" moment that could last a lifetime.

The moral of this scenario is that if a field trip isn't making the connections that you hoped—place a large stuffed animal in the middle of the path.

Experience: Visiting George Washington Carver's Home
Location: George Washington Carver (GWC) National Monument
Audience: Fourth-Grade Class
Educational Goal: Make Students Aware of the Challenges and Accomplishments of GWC

Scenario: One of the small gems of the National Park Service is the George Washington Carver National Monument in southwestern Missouri. School programs offered at this site are rich with a variety of interpretive media. Students in less than a day, are led through a well-planned interpretive trail, a special classroom session on peanuts, an innovative hands-on science center, and a visitor center tour and film.

Results: Students were interviewed 14 months after their field trip to the park to learn what they recalled from the half-day immersion into Carver's life and history. Their recollections reflected the mission desired by the park. However, one experience that seemed to leave all of the children in awe and a bit mystified was the original home of George Washington Carver. The students' visit in the house was only five minutes of the half-day experience, but its impact was apparent long after their brief visit.

> *I remember there was, like, a big wooden fence around the house and inside the*

A Tool to Promote Tolerance

The George Washington Carver National Monument is a 210-acre national monument that includes rolling hills, woodlands, and pasture. Within the monument are a half-mile interpretive trail, museum, interactive science laboratory, 1881 Moses Carver house, and Carver cemetery. One year following a field trip to this park, fifth-grade students were interviewed to learn what recollections and/or impacts occurred based upon their half-day visit. The most notable findings from these interviews were the potential long-term compassion for and/or understanding of Carver's achievements exhibited by the students. Students discussed recollections of Carver's lack of formal education and understood how he was treated as a youth because of his race.

THE CARVER HOUSE

> Yeah, just how he was black so he couldn't go to school, but then he ended up going anyway. They talked about how he wasn't treated very well and how sometimes the people were mean to him 'cause he was a different color and his parents were dead.

> He sat behind a schoolhouse and he watched the other children through the windows to read.

When asked by the researcher, why didn't he go inside? *Because the school didn't allow blacks.*

Upon exploring the remnants of an old tree that was once used to hang runaway slaves, the student explained: *My teacher and the ranger were telling us about a tree that they used to hang [runaway slaves].*

When asked about her feelings concerning this action the student replied: *Yeah, I think it's hatred. I don't think that they should have done that.*

These statements reflect not only recollections of Carver's challenges, but also potential views towards tolerance.

house, it was really crowded and there wasn't much space. I think there was an upstairs room. I wasn't sure cause there was a door that was locked.

Okay, so we went to George Washington Carver National Monument and, like, we walked around and saw his house and stuff. And it was small, like, really tiny and a ton of people had to live in that tiny house…. There wasn't room for all of them, but, like, they, like, had to all live there because they didn't have any money.

We got to go in his house, but we didn't get to go upstairs because they said the stairs were really old. And he built the fences.

We went to see a cabin, like, where he lived and where his parents lived. It had, like, a wagon there and like a little restroom on the side of the house. And the cabin was really small.

I liked his house the most because we got to see where he lived. It was like I was living with him.

The Carver field trip offered a variety of excellent educational strategies to convey the message of Carver and his life. But the novelty of the size of the tiny cabin became a vivid memory for the students, and strengthened their respect for Carver's challenges.

The Argument for Paying for a Bus

The high prices for bus transportation, coupled with the tremendous pressures of standardized testing, will only make it more difficult for schools to visit interpretive facilities. The best strategy to take on these daunting issues is to explain to the powers that be the cognitive and emotional value of such experiences. The results shared in this chapter, along with detailed findings in the associated research studies, can only help in the battle to bus the kids to resource sites.

- Investigating and discovering the geology of a region
- Learning the impact of invasive species on ecosystems
- Understanding the complexities of bird migration
- Discovering the predation patterns of reptiles
- Learning the geothermal process associated with volcanoes
- Developing empathy for other races and cultures

All of these educational outcomes (and many more) were achieved and proven through *long-term research*. It is the ammunition that can best be used to help pay for a bus.

7

The Interpreter

As governmental agencies go, the Park Service is a good one, far superior to most. This I attribute not to the administrators of the Park Service—like administrators everywhere they are distinguished chiefly by their ineffable mediocrity—but to the actual working rangers and naturalists in the field, the majority of whom are capable, honest, dedicated people.

—Edward Abbey, *Desert Solitaire*, 1968

I think that a major weakness with the National Park Service interpretation today is its over-emphasis on personal services interpretation.

—Sam Vaughn, *Journal of Interpretation Research*, 2004

Once upon a time, there was an assumption that when a visitor entered a resource site such as a national park, national forest, or state park the primary source of information—both desired and available—was a real, live interpreter. Today this could not be farther from the truth. As Vaughn notes, "About one in 20 National Park System visitors attend interpretive programs. Most visitors do other things. More than one-third visit visitor centers with exhibits and videos; more than that use brochures and read wayside exhibits." (p. 61, 2004). This percentage may even be wishful thinking. For example, in the most visited park in our country—Great Smoky Mountains National Park—visitors get out of their cars for a grand total average of 15 minutes. The Park Service is not alone in its lack of quality time with the human interpreter. All resource sites, from city to county, private to nonprofit, struggle with the cost benefits of interpreters versus signage, websites, and brochures. The latter are significantly cheaper and can reach more people. This dilemma has created a calling to move away from the emphasis in personal services interpretation to other approaches.

The purpose of this book was to learn, through research, what variables make up successful long-term interpretive outcomes. However, a funny thing happened through the 15 years of research and 25 studies conducted by the author. One of the most important influences on the visitor, from the studies conducted, was the flesh-and-blood interpreter. This certainly could be due to the focus on personal service assessment. However, the intense memories—some bad, but most positive—offer the notion that the person may be as important as the message. To some, especially at the federal level, this may not be what they want to hear, since getting the message of the agency to the people is vital to the profession's mission. But make no mistake, desired or not, the face-to-face contact with an interpreter is important.

Interpreter versus Non-Interpreter Services

When the flesh-and-blood interpreter is compared to the impact of other nonpersonal interpretive techniques, the results tend to reinforce the importance of the human factor. For example, a study on visitor experiences and media effectiveness in Rocky Mountain and Yellowstone National Parks showed the importance of the interpreter. As noted in the report:

> The friendliness and helpfulness of people at visitor center information desks was the strongest visitor center experience contributing to visitors' belief that they were valued by the National Park Service (NPS). Such perceived client support increased the likelihood that visitors would provide a quote for the NPS to use to promote park attendance…. Virtually no visitors reported unsatisfying experiences with NPS staff. Helpfulness of the park's staff plays a prominent role in visitors' beliefs that the NPS cares about their trip enjoyment and values their contribution to NPS's mission. (Eisenberger & Loomis, 2003)

But probably one of the stronger cases for the impact of the interpreter versus other media comes from an extensive review of a variety of interpretive techniques. *Visitor Use and Evaluation of Interpretive Media*, a report on visitors to the National Park System conducted by the National Park Service Social Science Program, analyzed data collected in 23 in-depth studies. Each of these studies had been conducted with specific emphasis on visitor use and evaluation of interpretive media. The goals of this analysis were to document visitor use and evaluation of various interpretive media, and compare the use and evaluation patterns of visitors based on various visitor and visit characteristics.

The analysis found that park brochures and visitor center exhibits were used by the largest proportion of visitors who reported use of interpretive media. Wayside exhibits and self-guided tours were used by one-third of visitors surveyed. Audio-visual programs, park newspapers, bulletin boards, park information radio stations, and park websites were each used by fewer than one-third of all park visitors surveyed. Finally, 22 percent of all park visitors surveyed reported participation in ranger-guided programs. However, interpreter-led programs ranked higher in importance and quality than almost all other interpretive media.

> Fewer than one-quarter of all visitors surveyed reported participation in ranger-guided programs. Those who did participate in ranger-guided programs considered them to be "very important." The quality of ranger-guided programs was consistently "good" as rated by those visitors participating in them. For visitors, ranger-guided programs are among the most important aspects of a park's interpretive offering. They are of the highest quality. Only on occasion was a type of interpretive media considered more important than ranger guided. (Forist, 2003)

Three studies from the author support these findings. These evaluations included both personal and nonpersonal interpretation and assessed long term recollections from visitors' experiences of both type of media.

Grand Canyon's Tusayan Museum
This study assessed the long term impacts of the museum's program titled, "Glimpses of the Past." Its subject matter is an interpretation of artifacts and culture of an abandoned 800-year-old Pueblo Indian ruin discovered near the south rim of the Grand Canyon. The first portion of the program took place inside the Tusayan museum and lasted for approximately 15 to 20 minutes. The program then proceeded outside for 25 to 30 minutes, during which visitors walked around the ruins on a looping trail facilitated by museum staff. Ten months following the experience, visitors were asked about what they recalled in the museum versus what the interpreter shared during the program. Responses regarding their recollection of the museum were broad in scope and did not reflect specific information from the exhibits and signage, with the exception of a large painting (see Chapter 2). In fact, many of the respondents, in answering museum-related questions, referred to the interpreter:

> *One theme was sort of the importance of archeology. I remember her talking about how they were glad the original archeologists left areas undisturbed on*

INTERPRETER AT ST. LOUIS ARCH MUSEUM/NPS PHOTO

purpose so that later people with additional technology could come back. The ground-penetrating radar they used to gather more information about the ruins that hadn't been disturbed earlier. So I thought that was very interesting.

This recollection was not of the museum, but rather, the interpreter talking about the theme of the site.

Jefferson National Expansion Memorial
A second study that was held in a museum that used both personal and nonpersonal interpretive techniques was at the Jefferson National Expansion Memorial at the St. Louis Arch. The programs were approximately 30 minutes in length and were led by an interpreter along with the opportunity for the participants to read and view exhibits and signage featuring aspects of the Lewis and Clark expedition. Ten months following these tours, visitors were interviewed to learn what recollections seemed to keep long after their experience. Recall of the museum's signage and exhibits was general at best. Below are representative comments about this interpretive media:

They had the pictures of the falls. I don't remember the name of the falls. They are in South Dakota. And at a certain time of the day or night, something with the moon or the sun reflects. It is really cool.

I think we might have actually been in front of, not a statue, but a wax figure of Lewis and Clark. But I think at one point there were wax figures dressed up, Lewis and Clark.

Just typical things that you see in a history museum—like a mock-up of a camp site and some of the animals. It seems like they had the utensils out, that they would use for camping at that time. And then there were maps of which states were entering the Union.

What we were standing in front of was a picture of, I want to say Louisiana Purchase. We were standing in front of one of a mural or something in front of us that talked about Lewis and Clark.

A lot of the pictures and stuff of Lewis and Clark expedition and stuff were kind of in that area and then they had props and stuff too.

On the other hand, recall of the interpreter and his or her actions during the program seemed to offer more vivid recall than the exhibits and signage.

He did have something at one point or he stopped at the end and had stuff. There was some point at the end where he took people over and there was some buffalo hides and stuff. But I think he did that at the end because there is nothing really next to the back wall. I think he did the back wall and then he hit some of the highlights.

The things I remember most about his presentation were the artifacts, I guess you would call them, he brought in. I remember he had a couple guns and some, like, clothing that they would wear. And like some other, I think he had some Indian stuff too. Yeah, he had them and you could hold them and try some of the costumes on and hold the gun up.

Yeah, he showed us how they would load the black powder. And he explained the coats. I remember he had, like, coats that were really thick thick wool. And they were really heavy and he just, like, showed us how they were made and how thick they were and all that sort of stuff. Everyone who wanted to try the coat on could try it on or hold the gun or, he passed a lot of things around. Oh, I remember he passed, like, a corn around. There was like a big money piece, probably twice the size of a half dollar. He showed us that.

She used, like, a chain to represent the chain of command. It was what Lewis and Clark had to follow and their expedition and how they used the chain of command and things like that.

He demonstrated how flint makes a spark with a piece of flint and a piece of metal, striking the one on the other.

I liked her presentation in the manner that she used visual effects. She used a chain. It was a link, a large link chain she had. And what she used it for was to describe the chain of command. Yes, and she was able to tell us how Lewis and Clark, one of them had some military background. And of course when they got their gentlemen all together for their trip, they had to have this, some sort of order in the group. So who was taking orders from whom, and so forth. And she explained it that they were in charge. And here were the other frontiersmen that came with them or were accompanying them and they had to understand that there was a chain of command and who was the leader and who, you know, what they required of the other men to do. So that was able to help. And so she said, "If you have this chain," that visual effect with the chain, "and how they linked together and they are strong. But if there is a weak link, the chain will collapse. It will break." So it was very helpful for her to explain that. And how the chain will work better; not so much side-by-side as it will in a diagonal movement. So she, I liked that. I liked also that she used uniforms and she had my son try on one of the uniforms.

In this assessment, the recall of the interpreter's actions far outweighed the recollection of the exhibits. In fact, the recall of the interpreter—for better or worse—was more vivid and detailed than the recall of the museum and its artifacts.

I remember that he was very informative. I remember being intrigued by it. It kept my attention during the entire time. Probably can't recite facts to you, but I recall that he was very informative and very interesting. I enjoyed it very much.

He seemed to be very personable. Asking questions. Trying to get the people to interact. Outgoing, trying to make people ask questions—open-ended questions you know. "What do you think?" "How would you feel?"

He was very direct. He was good with kids—that he got the kids involved that he spoke to. He gave them things they could touch and pull and move when it was appropriate. And he asked them questions and got them, he interacted with them.

I thought what he did was good, but the audience he had at the time I don't think had the patience to sit and watch, listen for that long. I think maybe he got a little bit too detailed. We had two kids there that were at the time, in kindergarten and first grade. And I think he might have gotten a little too in-depth.

The 30-minute guided tour of the St. Louis Arch Museum clearly showed that the guide had much more of an impact than the museum he or she was guiding them through.

George Washington Carver National Historic Monument
Of all the research conducted by the author, nothing demonstrates more of the value of the interpreter versus other interpretive strategies than a one-year post analysis of a school field trip to the George Washington Carver National Historic Monument. The administrators at the park were interested in learning the impact that a new, state-of-the-art science center had on students. The facility, although small, included an array of exhibits and signage that offered interactive experiences, intricate dioramas, and other high-tech delivery systems. Recollections from this four-hour field trip were primarily on target with the message about Carver and tolerance. (See Chapter 6.) However, the impact of the science center and its array of nonpersonal interpretive techniques showed very little impact, with only a handful of respondents recalling any of the "gadgets" in the center.

We got to press these buttons in a center room where stuffed wolves were and birds and you got to hear them chirp and they moved and stuff.

We looked on the computer and it had, like, um, like an animal scene set up, and you pushed the buttons and the animal, you had to find what animal made the sound.

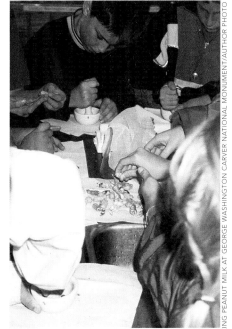

MAKING PEANUT MILK AT GEORGE WASHINGTON CARVER NATIONAL MONUMENT/AUTHOR PHOTO

On the other hand, a majority of students remembered the one interpreter-led activity conducted in the science center. This consisted of the ranger helping students make peanut milk.

Yeah, the ranger and the class crunched up peanuts. You didn't take anything off of them, you crunched them up. You put them in hot milk and stirred it up and it was ready, but you had to let it sit for a little while.

We got a partner and then we got these little white bowls with peanuts in them.

And then we got these sticks and crushed them up and we put like milk in them and we shook them up but we didn't have to drink it, thank God.

When the park contacted the author to help support the development of a larger science center they asked what should be included in the new building. My answer—interpreters.

Lasting Impressions

As the studies above suggest, the impact of interpreters—in the flesh—cannot be overstated. Their presence, both positive and negative, has been prevalent in all of the research conducted for this book. Below are lasting impressions visitors had of their interpreter, long after the program was over.

Like I said, the individuals that put it on were excellent and I would definitely recommend it to anybody, even if you don't have an interest in it—you definitely will once you sit through it because they just made it so that there were questions constantly going in your head as things were going on or you think, "Oh my gosh, I didn't know that." So I would definitely recommend to anybody because, like I said, even if you don't know anything about it, you will definitely know when you get out of there. (Brown County State Park Deer Program)

He was friendly. I thought he was very good. I thought he did a really good job with the tour. He got people interactive and interested and enjoyed that. And he made it very informatively interesting. He tried to get people to guess which picture was which, which was Lewis, which was Clark. He had people guessing sometimes like about why is it written like this? So it was really cool. (St. Louis Arch Museum Tour)

It was very entertaining, very engaging. … The woman that spoke for the most part was, like I said, very engaging and had a really nice style and good sense of humor. She really made it very exciting. … It just keeps everyone awake and light and extremely interested. The guide did a lot, I think, to include everybody on the tour in terms of engaging them in what was going on, which really is important. (Lowell Canal Boat Tour)

She acted like she was going to stand there, by golly, until everybody's questions got answered. She never gave you the feeling that she was trying to rush you or herd you along or that you were insignificant or that anything that you had to say was stupid or dumb or not important. Yes, she interacted with the crowd a lot. And I thought, especially for having done this over and over and over for hundreds of times, she made it feel like she was fresh and that it was the first time she had ever done it and that she just couldn't wait for us to learn everything that she had to tell us and, and she just, she was just wonderful. (Denali Dog Sled Program)

She must have known her material extremely well. I mean because, she believed what she was saying there. I mean, she was excited about it and she put some fun into it. It seemed like she took some ownership of what is going on out there and she was proud to be there as a ranger there in the park. (Denali Visitor Center Program)

He was very laid back. He was certainly very informative. He sort of went at a slow pace. He just sort of let us go down and just observed as we walked down. He was extremely knowledgeable. He was very personable. He was very attentive to the differing ages and ability levels and fitness of all of us there. He was very attentive, but kept the pace going. He knew that we wanted to see all these things and it didn't feel rushed, but he would kind of hold back and make sure that everybody had kind of gotten along. (Haleakala Rainforest Hike)

He told all those different little stories. … He told things in good, in little easy ways to remember, little stories he connected you with whatever you were looking at, which for me helps me remember. … He had a good way of telling a story. (Yosemite Tram Tour)

She was very good with the group as a whole. She took control of the group, because I know that being outside, you know, people had tendency to get up and do what they need to do, and kids are a little more apprehensive because it was at nighttime. She would just take control. (Hoosier National Forest Bat Program)

Of course, with the good can come the bad, and in our studies there were certainly some issues raised about the interpreter. But these observations were few and far between.

The main problem is that she spoke to us as though she were addressing a first-grade or second-grade class. … She was constantly interrupting instead of treating the tour as a mature, grown-up experience, which it was. … It was just her presentation needs to be age-appropriate.

I don't know if he was reading from a script or from memorizing a script. … I don't know how many, how long he's been doing that.

She got going and is one of those people that gets going, they can't stop. … She just kept talking, and it was, like, annoying after a while. … I had to just block her out.

It doesn't matter how good and beautiful the place is if the person can't make it come alive. … That's what they do, they make the place come alive, I guess is probably the succinct way of putting it.

Despite these comments, the overall impression from virtually everyone interviewed in our research saw the interpreter as valuable and a positive aspect of their visit to the resource site.

Yeah, she grabbed the crowd, got us involved in it, and made it come alive for us.

Do Interpreters Meet Their Own Expectations?
So far, this chapter supports the importance and lasting impressions that an interpreter may have on his or her visitors. However, do interpreters live up to their own goals for a program? Do the outcomes desired by professionals meet the recollections or impact exhibited by participants? Through the variety of research conducted for this book, both outcomes and interpreter goals have been compared in a variety of ways.

Interpreter Interviews
One approach to learn if an interpreter's goals were met was through interviewing them following the program to get a sense of what recollections or impact his or her participants might have months after the program. Below is a sample of such

The School Field Trip Effect

I don't know who was laughing more, the students or the parents accompanying the children on the field trip to Clingman's Dome in Great Smoky Mountains National Park. For the past 20 minutes, Ranger Mike was explaining the effects of acid precipitation on the forest of the region. It was certainly not a humorous subject, but one that he was able to make engaging and entertaining for all who were watching. His style and charisma were variables I felt certain would come through when the author would interview the students a year later. (See Chapter 6 for results.) But those recollections were not to be—nor were countless other memories that the researcher had of excellent interpreters leading school programs at their parks. The "power" of the ranger in school field trips (at least to the children interviewed) was overshadowed by the activities and experiences recalled from the program. Unlike the vivid and powerful impressions recorded by adults, the role of the interpreter for the children played much less of an influence.

I shared the "bad news" to Ranger Mike that the kids remembered the idea of air pollution but didn't even remember if their guide was a "he" or a "she." He thought that was fantastic. After all, he explained, the message is what he wanted them to leave with—not that he was a talented entertainer. And so it was, with virtually all school field trips assessed for this book. The rangers, no matter how personable, charismatic, or entertaining, were much less recalled than the experiences they were facilitating.

an interview for an interpreter who led the Denali dog sled program.

> Author: *For this specific program that you just did, what are things that you perceive that would be things that you think would be connections that would be made six months from now?*

> Interpreter: *Well, I'm hoping that they are going to remember that it takes a lot to manage a park and that it's a team effort. That was the number one thing. And the symbolization of team is not just the rangers, it's really the dogs. That's what I'd like them to remember is, is how the dogs work together as a team and that we couldn't run this park without those dogs. Those are some of the core concepts that I would like to be remembered.*

Below are some recollections from visitors of that same program, six months following our interview.

> *You realize that, you know, [the dogs] are basically working, it's not just a fun game thing where we are taking somebody for a ride or when they race to Nome. It's just a working life, and you say to yourself, it is so much better for the*

environment rather than running snowmobiles up and down the mountains. But they have dogs and it's really a history, it's a connection.

My husband and I both went away feeling how important the dogs have been through the history of the park, through getting them, enabling them to take care of the park in the inclement weather that they have.

It helps people like me who go, "Hey, they're doing some good here. They're not wasting taxpayer money or anything like that." That there's a good purpose behind having the dogs.

Another interpreter was interviewed at the same park regarding the impact she hoped to have on participants of a visitor center program. Again, below is a sample of the interview conducted by the author.

Author: *First of all, what did you want them to come away with?*

Interpreter: *I wanted them to see that there are lessons learned in the national parks. With animals, it's usually games and lessons taught by, you know, the parents or whatever, things that are learned that help them survive. With people, it's lessons that we've learned from history and trial and error to help the park survive. So it kind of boils down again to survival, but also to the lessons that will help with survival. It goes with animals but also with us.*

Author: *Any other sub-goals or objectives that you have with that program, that you were trying to achieve with it?*

Interpreter: *Yes, again, it is kind of broad because I am talking about five different animals. One of the goals is that three out of four people would identify with one of the games that one of the animals played. Not specifically with all of them, but particularly with one. Each one would remember one animal and the lesson they had learned to be able to survive.*

Responses 18 months following the program offered general recollections about the animals she talked about, but certainly her attempt to connect games of animals and people was not retained.

Honestly, what I picked up from it was that, like, the idea of things working together. I don't know if that is the right wording. Like for the animals that lived up there and how they got along day-to-day living next to each other, maybe.

What kinds of animals there were in the national park and she told us about what not to do in front of the animals.

Just to familiarize with the bear and the animals and the whole park area there and the whole ecosystem.

I'm pretty sure they just mainly talked about all the different animals and all about them.

In both cases, the outcomes desired by the interpreter were vaguely retained— certainly more for the first case than the latter. Obviously the recall isn't a cause for celebration, but it must be cautioned that these are responses from long after the program and their time with their participants lasted 30 to 40 minutes.

Park Goals and Mission
Another approach assessed to see if outcomes matched the desires of interpreters was to match interpretive goals and objectives with recollections of participants. Below are desired goals developed by park staff at George Washington Carver National Monument school programs.

Desired Futures Focusing on Interpretation
1. Expand and modify existing interpretive programs to provide for a greater **understanding** of GWC.

2. Manage cultural and natural resources to **memorialize** Carver's life in a dignified and inspirational setting.

3. Manage the park's **resources** so they can be used to help interpret how the boyhood farm and surrounding area influenced Carver's life.

4. Encourage the public to develop a deep understanding of Carver's achievements and **services to humanity**.

5. Explain the **historical context** in which Carver grew up and his efforts to get an education.

Students who participated in a school program with these goals were interviewed one year following their field trip, with responses that included the following:

He was black so he couldn't go to school, but then he ended up going anyway. They talked about how he wasn't treated very well and how sometimes the people were mean to him because he was a different color and his parents were dead.

He wrote a speech that persuaded people to believe that, uh, to persuade people that being slaves isn't the best thing in the world and to tell them that if you were a slave, would you like being treated like they did?

The separation of blacks and whites—like the blacks got the crappy toilets with all the mold growing up in it and the stinky seats, like the sewer water. And the white people got like the good faucets with nice, clean water…and like, the blacks had their own stinky restaurants and the whites had their nice five-star restaurants. Like, so we stop it and don't do that anymore…cause it wasn't the right thing to do and all.

While not meeting all of the park goals, responses from students certainly showed that their field trip to this site was well worth it in relation to what the interpreters wanted to see happen.

A second example offers a mission statement for a residential program at Yellowstone National Park. Certainly, the goals embedded in this statement reflect noble and worthy benchmarks and were concepts that were well delivered during the five-day program.

Our goal at *Expedition: Yellowstone!* is to encourage a philosophy and ethic which promotes stewardship of park, regional, and global resources by facilitating student groups in understanding their interrelatedness with the natural world.

One would hope that one year after this program, this mission was accomplished, but judging from these responses and others (see Chapter 6), understanding of resources was accomplished, but actual stewardship goals were not as evident.

I learned that steam is visible, water vapor is not.

That underground geysers are like plumbing systems. They start at the area where the water is and gets heated up by the earth's core.

That the wolves almost became extinct in Yellowstone and ones were reintroduced and people were saying that the wolf would ruin the ecosystem, but they didn't. They really helped them out because all the sick animals were taken by the wolves, which made the herds stronger.

The Bottom Line

The four assessments of desired versus actual outcomes suggest that what can occur in an interpretive program may be less than we would want. However, it is important to return to the main premise of this chapter, which is the importance of the actual interpreter. While, for example, the outcomes achieved by the Denali visitor center interpreter were not aligned with her hopes for the program, the impression made by her passion, leadership, and knowledge were more vivid and, in the end, just as important.

If I Knew Then What I Know Now

There were many questions I had about the impact of interpretation while spending 10 years in the field. Those questions led to my entrance into the academic world and my 15-year quest to attempt to answer those questions. And, hence, the preceding chapters are the author's results of those years of research, observations, and assessments. There are findings that are not earth-shattering and certainly support the leaders and trainers of interpretation. There are other findings, however, that seem a bit more surprising—both in good and not-so-good ways. Ultimately, the results of this work led to a summary of thoughts that I call "If I Knew Then What I Know Now." It is a list of findings and observations that seem to be key consistencies that would have helped me when I was planning or presenting interpretive experiences. Hopefully, they will help others in the future.

Freeman Was Right!
At least with his first principle, "Any interpretation that does not somehow relate what is being displayed or described to something within the personality or experience of the visitor will be sterile." Whether it be in a small group hiking through the forest with an interpreter, or sitting with 100 other visitors listening

to a campfire program—if the information was relevant to *their* lives the recollection or impact was far greater than otherwise. The rich findings from the Lowell Canal program versus the more general recall for the Yosemite tram tour offer support for this observation. Consistently, the participants interviewed after the Lowell programs were from the area and knew about people who worked in mills or had seen and been in mills before. Therefore, many had thorough recall related to the specific theme of the program. On the other hand, the Yosemite participants were from different states (and countries) with little or no previous experiences or connections to the park. Hence, recollections were general in nature, focusing on novel aspects, such as the rock climbers and the interpreters' styles of leading programs. The importance of this finding leads to the second area on this list.

Do What We Say, Not What We Do

Despite the overwhelming call for relating to the visitor and research supporting this notion, many interpreters observed for this book did *not* attempt to learn who the visitors were and/or their relationships with the topics at hand. It is clearly understood that this type of constructivist approach is much more difficult than simply offering pleasantries such as "Where are you from?" at the beginning of a program and then going into didactic mode. But occasional probing with the group—no matter what the subject matter—will do two things. First, it will reinforce to the visitor their ownership in the program and, second, aid the interpreter in *relating* the topic to his or her constituents. Is it so hard during a 45-minute campfire program to ask, "Does anyone have any bear encounters they would like to share?" Does this group management skill go beyond lecture tactics—you bet. But could it result in a longer lasting recollection or impact for the visitor—no question about it.

Interpretation Is an Episodic Event

Whether we like it or not, the interpretive experience for an individual is a small blip on his or her life's radar. We have them for 30 to 40 minutes—maybe longer or shorter in some cases—and then they're gone. Therefore, much of this research is based on human memory theory. Behavior change or persuasion models are important to consider with the hope that we can attain such goals. But let's not fool ourselves that a 30-minute encounter will be more than a memory. However, it is up to the field to include variables that will keep that recollection alive as long as we can, and maybe make it a memory that can create long-term impacts. Certainly, there were a handful of adults and even more children who seemed to walk away from their interpretive experiences with memories that instilled long-term interest for the site and/or subject to which they had been exposed. Examples such as a couple from the Yosemite tram tour that joined the park's association after the program and school students who, a year later, clearly had empathy for George Washington Carver's life and struggles to achieve his success are present in this book. But they are the exception and not the rule. This may not be what an interpreter wants to believe and, in fact, it may seem to be a pessimistic conclusion. On the contrary, it is a pragmatic way to view our impact. As shared throughout the book, visitors, both young and old, had incredibly rich, positive, and lasting memories, and those findings are ones that the interpreter can be proud to have created.

Each Park Has A "Hook"

As the research studies and the results continued to grow, the author found that resource sites had "hooks" or particular tangible/intangible variables that helped them create lasting impacts. These variables were physical objects such as Carver's home or Tusayan's large painting of Pueblo ruins. They were novel sightings such as Yosemite's rock climbers or sled dogs responding to interpreters at Denali. Or they were particular interpreter-led experiences such as a cup-and-straw activity representing the woolly adelgid's impact on the Smokies Fraser fir. Whatever they were, these hooks may not be what the park thought they would be. For example, the program staff at the Smokies never would have thought a 15-minute "filler activity" before lunch would take precedence in impact over three and a half hours of hiking to the top of Clingman's Dome. From the researcher's perspective, learning what a park's hook is should be one of the more important evaluation goals. Discovering a site's "portal" can help in planning more time and experiences around those important variables.

Hands-on!

This is one of those findings that could be considered common sense, but it is a finding that seemed to be one of the most pervasive for both children and adults. No study exemplified that more than the museum tours at the Jefferson Expansion National Memorial. The 30-minute tours were led by excellent interpreters and were rich with information and exhibits about Lewis and Clark and our country's westward expansion. But recollections six months after the programs were overwhelmingly sided toward the furs and other hands-on props the program leader had both adults and children touch. These results, along with many of the other studies, offer a challenge to the field. As a profession we would much rather have the visitor retain the key topics and themes of the program and not that they picked up an antler. But since this seems to be the cruel reality of hands-on materials, further work needs to done to integrate the "props" with the subject matter.

Methods Matter

Program themes must be integrated with dynamic, interactive, and relevant approaches. If not, the themes lose their long term impact. To be sure, several resource sites were able to offer programs that communicated themes that were retained in the long term. However, the techniques / experiences that brought the

theme to life were more important than an offering of key words and/or phrases. Several examples can be noted to prove the point:

- One of the finest attempts at offering a theme came from the Denali visitor center interpreter. The parallel of animals at play and children's games—using slides of her childhood—was simply superb. Unfortunately, virtually none of the visitors interviewed 18 months after the program recalled the theme and, if there was any retention regarding the topic, it was Denali animals in general. In fact, most recall was of *touching* antlers and furs.

- On the other hand, one of the most successful programs to carry over its theme was in the same park using a much more dramatic program tool—sled dogs. The results clearly indicate that the impact of seeing, hearing, and in some cases touching the dogs was the hook to carry the theme of the importance of dogs in Denali's history.

- A third example of the technique overriding the theme occurred with a study at the Hoosier National Forest. Since the Forest Service interpreter was also a graduate student with Indiana University, program themes and techniques were closely developed with the author. Despite thorough front-loading of the primary themes of the program with the students, the results of interviews four months after the program were consistent with other studies that saw the loss of theme retention. Below is a summary of the findings from this research that reflects the technique over content observation.

> An emerging theme that came from the analysis of the categories was that student actions formed the basis for recollection of the interpretive program and those actions were important in influencing knowledge and attitude. An experience that has students catching, looking, searching, chasing, acting, etc., will be more successful in its retention than a program that is didactic and passive.
>
> Passive experiences associated with the interpretive program had an opposite impact. Cognitive information such as ecological concepts, wilderness information, and environmental issue information was vaguely recalled, at best, and in many cases misunderstood or misinterpreted. (Knapp & Poff, 2001)

These examples are not offered to suggest themes should not be developed—of course they should. However, the research shows that if a theme is to carry with the visitor beyond the boundaries of the resource site, the techniques to convey this information should be viewed as being as important as the message. Most interpreters relied on mini-lectures and verbal diatribes to convey the theme. *In a majority of the studies, verbal sharing of themes resulted in little to no long-term retainment.*

FAMILY PROGRAM AT ST. LOUIS ARCH/NPS PHOTO

Children Are Conduits

As much as I despised family programs for the feeling of being a babysitter rather than an interpreter, these audiences seem to have a power that certainly goes under the idea of "If I Knew Then What I Know Now." Several of the research studies found that a primary variable for adults to gain long-term impact of a program was if their sons or daughters enjoyed the experience. The Brown County deer program and the Hoosier National Forest campfire program on bats were both examples of this transference of experiences. Parents may not have recalled much about the program content but they did share that their kids either enjoyed touching the furs at a deer program or were amazed that bats don't always suck human blood. And, so, if I were transported back 20 years ago, I would happily focus my interpretive program on the children nipping at my heels, knowing that their positive experiences would ultimately "rub off" onto their parents.

Time and Size May Not Make a Difference

One of the more surprising results from the research was the fact that long-term recollections and impacts were not diminished if the programs were shorter and with more people. On the contrary, some of the more poignant recollections came from programs that had large audiences and, in some cases, were shorter in duration. Two programs in the same park illustrate this paradox.

A *four-hour* interpretive walk in a rainforest with *six people* yielded these types of recollections:

> *I think it was knowing a little history of it, telling us why certain trees maybe survived and why certain ones didn't—the ruggedness of it.*

> *We walked, walking down, and as we walked down he would certainly take time to point out the different types of vegetation and the history of it.*

> *Maybe it was towards the ocean, yeah. We just sort of started walking down, down, down, and like I said as we were walking down, just pointing out the different types of vegetation.*

> *Certainly, I didn't see a lot of wildlife. Hopefully, we would see a bit more of that. And I guess small birds we saw. They certainly pointed them out to us.*

> *Well, I think that the group we were with, a lot of them were very keen in terms of the bird watching. They could see them and focus on them and point them out to us.*

A *40-minute* star program with *50 people* yielded these types of recollections

> *Well, I found it so incredible that [native Hawaiians] left from their original*

locations and traveled west in the kinds of boats that they did. They were able with some confidence to find places that they had heard about from previous people. I mean the Hawaiian Islands and the Sandwich Islands, or whatever they were called in the early days, are sort of out there in the ocean and they were able to find them. And without the use of modern navigation, they were able to do that.

The aspect that I remember was the Polynesian names for the constellations and then how navigators were able to determine longitude, which was a problem because they didn't have clocks or chronometers. And then they associated Polynesian myths for the formation of the constellations.

What I remember most about it was one gentleman talking about the technical aspects of astronomy and another talking about Hawaiian lore as it pertains to astronomy. And that was very interesting because I figure we should go up there and go stargazing and see the stars. But then they put the Hawaiian lore with it, it was very special. So that was really good.

There was a local figure who they worshipped over the generations who saved his wife or girlfriend from a sea monster or something. And that his story was told to the sky through generations. So he saved his wife and he did this from some sea monster and then the story is told through the eyes of the people telling the story years and years ago. They passed on through the generations through that story through astronomy.

The professor, whoever was leading it, the guy from the university, he started telling us about the stars that were out that night. And the main focus of his discussion was relating the stars back to the way the Indians or the local natives interpreted that. And I remember he pointed to different constellations and related stories from the, I guess it must have been the natives from the island, how they made up stories to go along with the constellation. And the one that, there was a story about a little boy who went swimming and there was something about the time of year when the sharks were in the water. And so they were relating something about the orientation of the stars with perhaps a dangerous time to go swimming because of the sharks.

As discussed previously, a suggestion for the recall of the star program was the novelty of the night sky in Hawaii. However, a four-hour walk in a rainforest on the same island would seem to be pretty extraordinary as well. In any case, the experience with less time and more people made much more of an impact than the four-hour hike with six people.

Be Pragmatic About Environmental Interpretation

It is our most desired outcome. It is why many interpreters (including the author) got into the business in the first place—to have the opportunity to share the wonders of nature to strangers and hopefully get them to become stewards of the site and maybe even beyond its borders. The research does not show this long-term stewardship change. It does show new understandings and potential attitude changes, but not to the extent that any of us would like to achieve. It doesn't mean that it doesn't happen and that we shouldn't continue this noble mission. But it should temper our strategies and perhaps direct more attention on particular audiences. For example, as discussed in Chapter 4, research seems to show an important link between positive environmental behaviors and early family experiences. Therefore, it would make a great deal of sense to offer more family-oriented opportunities at the resource site that would hopefully be applicable to topics and skills that could be incorporated back at the home front.

Another important observation is that due to the brevity of contact with visitors, interpreters should focus on entry-level variables to environmental behavior change. These include ecological understanding, sensitivity to the surroundings, and general impacts that can be caused by humans. As noted in Chapter 4, opening a Pandora's Box can have an opposite effect—especially with children—and make visitors more confused and/or frustrated than empowered. In sum, if I knew then what I know now, I would give my audience the experience of seeing a sunset from a ridge top rather than fill 40 minutes with ecological topics, human impacts on that ecology, and ways to overcome global warming—which I did 20 years ago.

Roving Is Underrated

A park that does not have an aggressive roving strategy is missing important visitor connections and diminishing the power of the interpreter. *All* of the parks associated with this book under-utilized this technique. There are many reasons for this, including a lack of budget and more effort and resources directed toward traditional techniques. But, as noted in Chapter 5 and reiterated in this summary, the power of the flesh-and-blood interpreter cannot be ignored. Hence, having an interpreter milling around a popular overlook or walking a highly used path will offer more direct contact with the visitor, increase the odds of a quality experience for the visitor, and add viability for the use of interpretation at that resource site. More importantly, in administrative terms, it would make more economic sense for those hours to be amongst the people rather than spent in the back of a visitor center preparing for a program. Ultimately, the program would provide contact with fewer people than if he or she was setting up a "prop" near a major trailhead that was designed to catch bears, but would actually catch the most important prey—visitors.

INTERPRETER ROVING AT GREAT SMOKY MOUNTAIN NATIONAL PARK AUTHOR PHOTO

School Field Trips Are Winners

This is another observation that seems common sense. But the extensive research conducted for this book on the long-term impact of school field trips places it higher than many other interpretive experiences. However, these findings offer two important conditions that can even further the longitudinal recollections of these resource site visits. First and foremost, there seems to be more of a long-term impact on students who participated in pre- and post-trip experiences. Although this too is not a revelation, the differences between students who were prepped and debriefed and the schools that did little to prepare or enhance their field trip was substantially more significant than the author expected. As someone who led scores of field trips, the author is well aware of the challenge to get schools to accomplish viable pre- and post-experiences. So, more innovative approaches to ensure school cooperation need to be investigated. Possibly, the findings from the studies offered in this book can help convince teachers to become more involved.

A second finding that may be a bit harder to swallow is that virtually any information that was given in a didactic or passive approach was lost shortly after programs were completed. Field trips—even with four-month post-interviews—offered little significant content retention if not associated with active, hands-on experiences. For example, information imparted verbally during a hike or at a particular area was not retained. However, information associated with hands-on, active experiences was recalled. Below are examples of these types of recollections from a variety of field trips:

> *They divided us into groups with, like, there were like maybe three or four people in each group, and they gave us each a rock and a little bit to look at it to figure out what it was. We discussed it as a group and then at the end, everybody had to stand up and say what they thought it was. And she, she'd explain it and tell us whether we were right or wrong and why each rock was what it was and like how old it was and, like, how it was formed.*

> *Yeah, we crushed up soybeans and made milk and we got to drink it if we wanted some. Yeah, we, you crunched up peanuts. You didn't take anything off of them, you crunched them up. You put them in hot milk and stirred it up and it was ready, but you had to let it sit for a little while.*

> *[A leaf] was lying on the ground and we picked it up and we colored it and then we laid it under, actually we laid it under a piece of paper and then colored on top of the paper with the leaf on it and made, like, a little imprint.*

One of these active strategies that seemed to be very successful in creating long-term memories was the use of games. One game that involved diving to the ground elicited this reaction:

> *It was my favorite part of the trip because it was informative while you had fun playing a game that you know how to do.*

In viewing these responses, the recall of specific content is still general, but it represents much more concise recollections than verbal messages that had been offered by the interpreter. These findings (that were consistent with the 14 field trips studied for this book) set up another important challenge for interpreters. The more content integrated in the active experience or game, the higher probability that this information would carry along with the memory of the game. No better example of the success of the message with the activity was the straw-and-cup activity conducted during a field trip at Great Smoky Mountains National Park. Not only could students recall the activity, but they also understood the destructive abilities of the woolly adelgids on Fraser firs—one year later. Several other activities and games from a variety of field trips were able to achieve this integration. However, many students could only recall the action and not the point of the experience. So, ultimately, the extensive field trip findings suggest that there should be less talk at students and more experiences with students that infuse important program content.

Importance of the Interpreter
The results of the research in this book offer strong support to keep personal-

service interpretation. Despite growing pressure for less costly and more efficient interpretive strategies, the visitor regards the interpreter as one of the most important and certainly most memorable parts of a park visit. So whether leading a large campfire program or answering a visitor's question on a trail, it is important to understand that this personal interchange supercedes any signage, exhibits, or website the visitor may encounter.

Words Versus Numbers

One of the most popular questions asked by park administrators and/or supervisors of interpretation is how can their program be evaluated. The response from this book is that words speak for themselves. There is no question that quantitative approaches to program assessment—such as on-site surveys—may carry more weight due to the statistics involved. They also may be able to reach more people due to their brevity and convenience. However, they don't answer the questions that park interpreters want to know: What works and why? Hence, through 15 years of program analysis (a third being quantitative and the rest qualitative), it has been this researcher's experience that interviewing people— either one-on-one or in focus groups—has been the most meaningful and helpful. The inherent weaknesses of this approach highlight its strength. Qualitative assessments are difficult to generalize beyond a single research site. But, as noted previously, each park has its own hooks and its own stories. Therefore, to the supervisors or programmers who want to know whether their interpretive experience had any impact, this researcher suggests taking the time to contact constituents a week, a month, or a year after the program and learn, in their own words, what they recall, what they liked and didn't like, and what made the most impact. It is not as simple as having them complete a questionnaire at the end of a program, but the findings will be much more valuable.

A Final Word

There is no better job than that of an interpreter—an occupation that offers the chance to share with others the wonders of natural, cultural, and historic sites. However, it is a profession that has been predicated on the writings of a handful of individuals. In particular, Freeman Tilden wrote six principles that he believed to be the foundation for successful interpretation. Others followed his work to add to the base of interpretation. Leaders such as Grant Sharpe, Sam Ham, Doug Knudson, and others wrote seminal works in theory and methods regarding interpretation. But, as stated from the outset of this book, the field has offered little research-based material that can help practitioners and administrators understand the actual impacts of the profession and, more importantly, learn approaches that seem to be the most successful to attain desired outcomes.

As a practitioner of this profession for a decade, it was frustrating to know that interpretive literature and subsequent training programs were based on personal premises and theories related to interpretation but never based on facts from the field. This book is an attempt to offer these missing pieces—not as an end but as a beginning in the hope that others may add further research to a profession that can only be helped through this approach. In the end, much of what was discovered only solidifies principles and goals developed previously. But some of this work offers new directions in interpretive methods that could further enrich our outcomes. Whether reinforced principles or new premises, the results from this work help clarify what all of us want—long-lasting recollections and positive impacts of our preciously short interludes with the visitor.

Appendix: The Research

The following section outlines the research studies that were conducted and used for this book. They are placed in four categories for reference purposes: 1) Traditional Interpretation Research, 2) Large Group Interpretation Research, 3) School Field Trip Research, and 4) Model Development Research. These studies were all conducted with the support—both financial and staff—from Indiana University. They also would not have been possible without the financial support from the following agencies / organizations:

- National Park Service
- United States Forest Service
- National Park Foundation
- National Environmental Education and Training Foundation

The overview of each study outlines a brief description, the research design, and a summary of results. Where publication of study is not cited, the work is either an unpublished research report or in the process of being published. Finally, the studies are listed in chronological order beginning with the most recent.

Traditional Interpretation Research

Case Study Analysis of Interpretive Programs at Selected National Park Service Units

This study investigated and identified elements associated with successful interpretive programs through assessing what are perceived as important elements by interpreters in five U. S. national park units. This qualitative research study employed a multiple case study design to investigate variables associated with successful interpretation. The case study sites were decided on the basis of representation of a variety of park unit characteristics. Parks were chosen by the breadth and depth of personal service interpretation provided by the particular unit. Criteria were also based on the variety and types of programs offered to ensure the researchers a full range of program staff and offerings. This information was gained through the aid of the Chief of Interpretation Office of the National Park Service. The units included a major western site (Yellowstone), a major eastern site (Great Smoky Mountains), a mid-range park (Shenandoah), an urban unit (Cuyahoga), and a historical park (George Washington Carver).

Research Design

A triangulation method was employed to collect multiple sources of data to control for possible biases caused by the researcher being the sole observer. Data sources included: semi-structured interviews with interpretive personnel, analysis of documentation related to interpretive programs in the units, and participant observation of interpretive programs conducted at each site.

Data attained from interviews reflect responses from a series of open-ended questions examining elements believed to contribute to a successful interpretive program. A total of 35 interviews was conducted from the five park units. The general criterion used to select the interview participants of the case studies was that they be full-time employees of the National Park Service who had interpretation as their primary duty. These positions ranged from field interpreters to chiefs of interpretation. All interviews were tape-recorded and later transcribed, word for word, for subsequent analysis. Descriptors, topics, values, and other issues were identified. This data was then categorized and assessed for relationships until distinct themes and sub-themes emerged.

Agency documentation and program observations were used to supplement the information gathered from the interviews. Each park unit shared key documents regarding the planning, development, and implementation of the unit's interpretive programs. Through an initial analysis of all materials, 10 specific forms of documents were selected for each park unit. These were the long-range interpretive plans, organizational charts, interpretive service inventory, representative newsletter, school program lesson plans, teacher surveys and curriculum evaluations, annual interpretation reports, visitor survey cards, school program evaluation forms, and visitor surveys and studies. A range of interpretive goals, techniques, and strategies is represented in this documentation. The author analyzed these supporting materials to correlate this information with the data generated from the interviews. Twenty-one public interpretive experiences at the five national parks were observed by the researcher as a third source of data. Interpretive venues observed included campground/campfire programs, interpretive walks, visitor center programs, site-oriented programs, and visitor center front desk interface. Focused note taking was employed to attempt to gain as much information from these events as possible.

All three sources of evidence (participant interviews, documentation analysis, and participant observation) were reviewed and analyzed together so that the findings were based on the convergence of the data collected.

Results

From the analysis of the data, four themes emerged. These themes reflect the researchers' interpretation of the data. Two of these general areas were consistently cited: (a) an interpretive program must relate to the visitor, and (b) it must attempt to achieve its goals through innovative techniques. Two other themes less emphasized in the data, but still prevalent, were: (c) the attainment of basic program needs, and (d) community outreach.

Participants in the study frequently attributed the success of an interpretive program to whether or not it connected with the visitors. In all park units, interpreters believed that connecting visitors to their message and their resource was crucial. In attaining this connection with the visitor, interpreters noted that "reading" the audience was crucial. Many interpreters interviewed believed that the relationship to the visitor would be strengthened through a direct connection to the park resources. Achieving this outcome would enhance the actual meaning for the visitor. Documentation analysis showed similar interest in promoting a strong relationship between the park and the visitor by way of the interpreter.

All interpreters who were interviewed related that a successful interpretive program must offer participants innovative techniques that would aid in accomplishing program outcomes. When describing innovative techniques, interpreters consistently and emphatically noted that the program must not become a lecture. Follow-up questioning by the researchers revealed that virtually all respondents associated this term with a traditional didactic technique. Lecturing was the single-most mentioned technique that impeded an interpretive message. A majority of interpreters wanted their programs to be interactive and considered these approaches to be innovative. All respondents felt it important that their constituents be actively involved during a program. Data from these interviews consistently pointed to successful programs as being very interactive and hands-on, rather than lecture-based.

Beyond the importance of relating to the visitor through innovative techniques, this analysis found that interpreters saw other program factors as being important to the successful outcomes of an interpretive program. Ability of the interpreter, program theme, and relationship to the park's mission are all considered basic program needs by the interpretive profession that were cited by most of the participants in this study.

A component considered necessary for a successful park-wide interpretive plan was the use of community outreach. Respondents from all five park units felt that community outreach was a vital aid to their current interpretive options and was a strategy that should be further developed. Specifically, community outreach was considered most crucial with the parks' gateway communities. The majority of comments promoting community outreach were associated with different ways to improve formal school program delivery.

Publications Related to Research
Knapp, D.H. (2005). The case for a constructivist approach to interpretation. *The Interpreter*. National Association for Interpretation: Fort Collins, Colorado.

Knapp, D.H., & Benton, G. (2004). Analysis of interpretive programs at selected
    national park service units: Variables for successful interpretation. *Journal of
    Interpretation Research, 9*(2), 9-25.

Knapp, D.H. (2003). Interpretation that works. *Legacy 14*(6), 26-33.

Interpretive Tour at a Historic Preservation Site

The interpretive site for this research was the West Baden Springs Hotel, located
approximately two hours south of Indianapolis, Indiana. The structure was
designated as the "eighth wonder of the world" in the early 1900s for its massive
dome structure, which was not eclipsed in size until the construction of the
Houston Astrodome. This study looked at the impact of a one-hour tour of the
facility immediately after and six months following the experience. The program
was a classic tour, in the sense that the interpreter led participants through the
hotel and grounds while offering information and stories related to the building
and its history. Fifty-three participants participated in the study, which was begun
in the summer of 2006, with all completing pre- and post-questionnaires, and
then 19 participating in informal, in-depth interviews.

Research Design

This study utilized a multi-method approach of analysis. The first assessment was
through a quantitative pre- and post-test administered at the site. The second
assessment was interviews conducted with a sample of the original population six
months after the experience. For the pre- and post-test, participants were asked to
respond to prompts using a Likert scale of 1 to 5 (1=Strongly Disagree,
2=Disagree, 3=Undecided, 4=Agree, 5=Strongly Agree). The questions consisted
of statements associated with the hotel and the supporting foundation behind its
renovation. Data was analyzed and subjected to the repeated measures T-test using
SPSS statistical software at the .01 level.

The qualitative assessment was initiated by the collection of in-depth
interviews from 20 participants. Participants were interviewed between six to
seven months following their visit to the hotel. A variety of prompts were utilized
to gain an understanding of what the participants experienced during the tour.
Questions such as "What did the tour guide tell you about the hotel?" and "Did
the person discuss any of the history about the place?" were used to solicit visitor
feedback. Ensuing statements or questions that stemmed from participants'
responses were utilized in an attempt to clarify the participants' discussion of the
experience. Interviews remained unstructured and participant-centered in order
to promote participant control of the interview's direction. To analyze the data,
the researchers transcribed the interviews and examined each individually
through a phenomenological analysis. Clusters of themes were referred back to
the original interview data in order to validate the subjective responses, and a
description of the phenomena resulted from the analysis.

Results

The quantitative assessment SPSS reports indicated that a significant difference was detected among the 53 participants between the pre-test and post-test. Scores showed change in knowledge between mean scores of the pre-test and post-test. In other words, specific content relating to the hotel and its history were retained immediately following the program.

The six-months-post interviews yielded four general themes. Recollection related to these themes was most vivid if the participant had some type of connection with the topic.

Architectural and Atrium Impressions

The recollections recalled by all 20 participants were memories regarding the 100-foot-high atrium and architectural uniqueness of the West Baden Springs Hotel. Participants most often discussed the atrium itself; however, many went into moderate details regarding the size and "awe-inspiring" presence the facility.

Craftsmanship

Impressions and memories regarding the craftsmanship of the hotel and grounds were recalled by 18 of the 20 participants interviewed. Common categories of recollection entail the ornate fireplace, golden leaves painted on the base of the interior columns, original work still present, statues, inlaid tile floor, and wood trim work.

General History

Twelve participants did recall historical information regarding the facility. Common topics consisted of recollections regarding the Jesuit occupation of the facility, spring wells, Northwood Culinary Institute, original wooden structure, gambling during the Prohibition era, and Al Capone's visits to the hotel and valley.

Tour Impressions and Recollections

Tour impressions and recollections regarding the tour's intricacies was the fourth-most cited theme. For example, 10 individuals discussed the interpreter and interpretation tour. All comments regarding the tour and the interpreter appeared to be of a positive nature.

Jefferson National Expansion Museum Tours

This study evaluated the impact of a guided tour of the Jefferson National Expansion Memorial Museum. The exhibits are dedicated to the history of Lewis and Clark and the western expansion of the United States. In an attempt to highlight aspects of the museum, the park offers interpreter-led tours of the exhibits, which focus on the Lewis and Clark expedition and other cultural and historical aspects of that era. The 30-minute tours use a variety of visual aids, props, demonstrations, and audience interaction. In September 2006, a research associate observed several of the tours and collected participant names. A list of 34 participants was generated from the visit.

Research Design

Five months later, researchers began calling visitors to set up post-program telephone interviews. Twenty-three visitors were interviewed, with their conversations tape-recorded and transcribed. The informal interview was initiated with the following statement: "Can you tell me what you remember about the ranger-led tours of the Jefferson National Expansion Memorial Museum?" A variety of prompts were utilized to gain an understanding of what the participants experienced during the tour. Interviews remained unstructured and participant-centered in order to promote participant control of the interview's direction. To analyze the data, the researchers transcribed the interviews and examined each individually through a phenomenological analysis using NVivo coding software, utilizing open and axial coding. Clusters of themes were referred back to the original interview data in order to validate the subjective responses, and a description of the phenomena resulted from the analysis.

Results

Four categories emerged from the coding and analysis of data. The richest and most abundant topic was props and demonstrations. In fact, the first recollection at the start of the interview for several participants contained references to props used by the ranger and held or worn mostly by children visitors. The second category to emerge related to the ranger and his or her presentation ability and style. With few exceptions, most of this recall was positive. A third major category was general information retained pertaining to the country's western expansion and the Lewis and Clark expedition. A fourth and broader theme was the positive comments associated with the visit and the tour. Although none was very specific, virtually all visitors interviewed left with more of a appreciation of the museum, its topics, and the interpreters.

Haleakala Rainforest Hike

This study conducted a longitudinal analysis of a half-day Haleakala Rainforest Hike two and a half years following the experience, which was during the summer of 2004. The original number of participants experiencing the hike was six, with two being interviewed for this study. The hike offered participants four hours of hiking through rainforest and other ecosystems representative of the island of Maui. The program was a classic interpreter-led program, in the sense that most of the time was spent hiking and stopping at particular points for information sharing by the interpreter. Most of the information was focused on wildlife and vegetation of the region, with some discussion of invasive species issues related to the Hawaiian Islands.

Research Design

A phenomenological analysis was conducted on the qualitative interview data from the two participants two and a half years after the hike. Interviews remained unstructured and participant-centered in order to promote participant control of the interview's direction. The transcriptions were processed using NVivo coding software to delineate categories and themes from the interview data. The researcher evaluated the phrases, categories, and themes, examining each by cross-checking the findings for internal consistency and delineating essential relationships among the themes. The small number of respondents is a clear limitation to this study. However, they represent a third of the program participants and their responses were consistent in recollection.

Results

Data from the interviews was consistent in offering fairly detailed description of the experience of the hike. In essence, both participants were able to describe some of the ecosystems they walked through and a stop in the "gully." However, this recall was general, with little to no specific content retained. The most specific topic recalled was the issue of invasive species but, again, retention was very general. This is important to note, since much of the hike had the interpreter sharing a great deal of information pertaining to the natural history and ecology of the area. A second area of general recall was associated with the other members of the group, such as mannerisms and involvement with the rest of the group. This area of retention was unlike other recollections from studies conducted. An assumption is that the length of time with the small group aided in this finding. In sum, the longitudinal memory for these participants was more of the hike and the group and not on specific content shared during the hike.

Haleakala Star Program

This study assessed the impact of a star program at Haleakala National Park. The higher elevations of Haleakala offer some of the best opportunities in the world for star gazing. So, not surprisingly, astronomy programs are a mainstay for interpretation at the park. Participants of these star gazing programs lay in the middle of a mountain meadow as two interpreters offered both fact and stories related to the major constellations and the secrets of Polynesian navigation. A unique aspect to the Haleakala star program was the tandem approach of a ranger sharing astronomy and a native Hawaiian sharing local stories associated with the constellations. In September 2004, the researcher observed the program and acquired eight participant contacts for follow-up interviews.

Research Design

A phenomenological analysis was conducted on the qualitative interview data from seven of the participants two and a half years after the evening program. The informal interviews were initiated with the following statement: "Can you tell me what you remember about the star program at Haleakala National Park?" Interviews remained unstructured and participant-centered in order to promote participant control of the interview's direction. The transcriptions were processed using NVivo coding software to delineate categories and themes from the interview data. The researcher and the research assistant then evaluated the phrases, categories, and themes, examining each by cross-checking the findings for internal consistency and delineating essential relationships among the themes.

Results

Three major categories emerged from the data. Each of these themes was found to be quite vivid for the length of time that had transpired since the interpretive experience. One primary theme was the recall of the use of stars for navigation and the mythology associated with this area. Recollections from the majority of interviews offered fairly specific information pertaining to some of the myths, which included reiterating, in general terms, a popular Hawaiian fable of a shark in the sky and it being a warning not to go in the water when that constellation is in the sky. A second area of significant recall was general folklore and legends associated with the Hawaiian culture. Several participants were able to iterate stories, in general to specific terms, that were told by the interpreters. These were separate from the mythological stories and were general folk stories told by the native, who was one of the leaders of the program. A final theme was the overall and significant positive impression the experience had on the visitors. This was related to the content of the program and its educational value, the setting, and the sharing of the experience with family members. Impressions of the program, in a positive tone, were some of the strongest seen from any of the research studies—due, in particular, to the longitudinal nature of the analysis. Overall, this study offers some of the richest long-term recollections of any studies conducted by the author.

Tour of Grand Canyon's Tusayan Museum

This analysis looked at long-term recollections of visitors who participated in a Grand Canyon's Tusayan Museum program titled "Glimpses of the Past" during the summer of 2005. Its subject matter was interpretation of artifacts and culture of an abandoned 800-year-old Pueblo Indian ruin discovered near the south rim of the Grand Canyon. The first portion of the program took place inside the Tusayan Museum and lasted for approximately 15 to 20 minutes. The program then proceeded outside for 25 to 30 minutes, during which visitors walked around the ruins on a looping trail facilitated by museum staff. Forty visitors were interviewed by telephone six to eight months after the program.

Research Design

Researchers utilized a phenomenological qualitative approach in an attempt to understand visitors' long-term memories of an interpretive program. Interviews were audio-taped and transcribed verbatim. Semi-structured interview questions began with open-ended questions following a flow of direction determined by the visitor. Follow-up questions were used to probe for richer explanations of the phenomena. Transcriptions were entered into NVivo 2.0 qualitative coding software and analyzed side-by-side by two researchers through two phases of coding. The phenomenological data was analyzed for specific language indicating information, impressions, topics, themes, contextual references, and conceptual learning.

Results

Two patterns developed from the analysis. The first pattern discovered was the recollection of museum and program information and content. One of those themes regarded the importance of archeology. A majority of respondents recalled the impact of seeing the ruins and noting the importance of uncovering those sites through archeology. A second theme under program information was visitors' respect and admiration for the people who lived during that time period. The second pattern discovered was recall of Indian culture and ruins enhanced by artist Roy Andersen's painted rendition of the community pueblo as it may have looked 800 years ago. A majority of respondents recalled the painting as an aid to the mental image of the village that would have been at the location of the ruins.

Canal Boat Tour of Lowell National Historical Park

The interpretive program analyzed was a canal boat tour program offered at Lowell National Historical Park located in downtown Lowell, Massachusetts. During the canal boat tour program, visitors rode in a small boat with an interpreter. They traveled along a stretch of canal, through a lock chamber, and onto the Merrimack River, then doubled back the way they came. Tour topics included the industrial revolution, mill operations, the role of the river and canals in powering the mills, immigrants, laborers, natural history, historic preservation, and ways in which Lowell has changed over the years. Ten canal boat tour programs were used for this study. These programs were led by six different interpreters over the course of four days in August 2004. A sample of 36 visitors was selected to be interviewed. The sample size represents approximately 25 percent of the total number of visitors participating in the 10 programs.

Research Design

Six months following the canal boat program, 36 participants were contacted by phone. The open-ended and unstructured interviews began with the following statement: "Could you please tell me what you can recall about the canal boat program that you participated in six months ago at Lowell National Historical Park?" Subsequent statements or questions represented attempts to obtain clarification or elaboration regarding the participants' experience. Interviews were participant-centered, in the sense that participants controlled the direction of the interview, including the subject matter and the range of topics discussed. The responses were transcribed verbatim for each subject and a phenomenological analysis was conducted. Each transcript was analyzed for phrases that described any memory a participant had from the program and his or her trip to the park. Such coded memories included everything from scenic viewpoints, major concepts, general or specific information from the program, emotions, ranger attributes, connections with other parts of respondents' lives, and recollections of other visitors encountered during the program. Second, emergent topic areas were identified from the clustering of similar coded memories through a constant comparison approach.

Results

Analysis of the interview data through the steps outlined above resulted in four topic areas relating to the recollections of the canal boat programs at Lowell National Historical Park. These were: personal connections with the tour, program information retention, positive visitor responses, and ranger attributes.

Personal Connections with the Tour

A predominant topic area that was found in the interviews of the canal boat tour participants was connections that were made during the program relating to their own personal experiences. In a setting such as Lowell National Historical Park, many of the visitors were familiar with the area, had relatives who were connected with some of the main themes discussed during the program, or had personal connections with Lowell and New England. These characteristics seemed to enhance recall of particular aspects of the program. One aspect of personal connection to the program was familiarity of the site and/or region. Twenty-two of the 36 interviewed offered an array of connections to the area. In recalling their memories from the canal boat tour program, respondents also mentioned their familiarity with friends or ancestors who had worked in mills. An important topic in the canal boat program is the story of the immigrants who came to this country and who were crucial to the success of the mills. Another personal connection that was exhibited through the interviews was close family members that lived in Lowell. Eleven of the 36 respondents mentioned such connections.

Program Information

A second major topic area that emerged from the interviews was specific information related to the interpretive program. Twenty-seven respondents mentioned different aspects of the Industrial Revolution, which was a primary topic of the interpretive program. The human history side of the Industrial Revolution was also recalled by 26 of the respondents. These recollections took on a decidedly empathetic view toward the people of the time and the struggles they went through. Beyond information related to the

Industrial Revolution and the people that were part of that history, the respondents also recalled specific tangibles associated with the tour and information related to them. For example, 25 respondents had strong recollections associated with the lock system that the canal boat actually went through.

Positive Visitor Responses
This topic area encompassed visitor reactions and emotional statements and reflections made in response to the memories recalled during the telephone interviews. Consistently, with virtually each responder, positive recollections of the program were conveyed. The most predominant category under this theme was general positive reactions to the tour. Thirty-four out of the 36 reported a general positive response to the tour. The positive reaction toward the program carried on beyond the actual tour itself. Thirty-three out of the 36 mentioned post-program actions that were related to their positive experience.

Ranger Attributes
A final topic that emerged from this study was the recollection of the interpreter who was leading the canal boat programs. Twenty-four of the 36 respondents offered unsolicited comments or recollections related to the interpreter. Many remarked on a variety of different communication skills associated with the interpreter. Along with the communication skills, 20 of the respondents were impressed with the interpreters' other qualities.

Publication Related to Research
Knapp, D.H. (2006). The development of semantic memories through interpretation. *Journal of Interpretation Research, 11*(2), p. 21-35.

Large Group Interpretation Research

Denali National Park Sled Dog Demonstration
This study evaluated the long-term impacts of Denali National Park's sled dog program. Each year, an estimated 50,000 visitors attend the interpretive program to learn about the use of sled dogs in Denali. The dog sled program is housed at a site that includes a historical museum, dog kennels, and a small arena for interpreter talks and dog sled demonstrations. The participants for this study were tourists who visited Denali National Park and who had arrived at the site by selecting to participate in the hour-long program and tour. During the program, participants had an opportunity to pet the dogs, visit the museum, talk with roaming rangers, and attend a 30-minute ranger discussion and demonstration about the historical and modern usage of the sled dogs in the park.

Research Design

A phenomenological analysis was conducted on the qualitative interview data from 32 participants who attended the formal ranger program at Denali National Park during the summer of 2004. Participants were interviewed between eight to 10 months following their visit to the program. The informal interview was initiated with the following statement: "Can you tell me what you remember about the dog sled program at Denali National Park?" A variety of prompts were utilized to gain an understanding of what the participants experienced at the park. Interviews remained unstructured and participant-centered in order to promote participant control of the interview's direction. To analyze the data, the researchers transcribed the interviews and examined each individually through a phenomenological analysis. Transcriptions were analyzed in three phases. The transcriptions were processed using NVivo coding software, utilizing open and axial coding. The second phase consisted of clusters of data being organized from the statements. This allowed for the emergence of themes common to all the participants interviewed. Clusters of themes were referred back to the original interview data in order to validate the subjective responses, and a description of the phenomena resulted from the phenomenological analysis. The researcher and the research assistant then evaluated the phrases, categories, and themes, examining each by cross-checking the findings for internal consistency and delineating essential relationships among the themes.

Results

Analysis of the interview data through the three phases outlined above resulted in the emergence of four themes from the participants' experiences at the Denali National Park sled dog program. These themes were: 1) knowledge retention, 2) the provocation of an emotional experience, 3) perceived change in attitude, and 4) empathy towards the dogs and/or rangers that work with the dogs.

> *Knowledge Retention*
> Vivid knowledge retention was noted throughout 26 of the 32 interviews. Participants primarily recalled information regarding the sled dogs, their use in patrolling the park, and the care of the animals, followed by information relating more holistically to Denali National Park. Other participants frequently recalled the usefulness of the dogs in maintaining the park.

> *Emotional Experience*
> Emotions that were prompted by the dog sled program were found throughout the interview data. Participants felt emotions of amazement and appreciation. Other recollections described a sense of spiritual experiences, isolation, solitude, respect, and need for stewardship.

Perceived Attitude Change

Perceived attitude change can be noted through some of the transcribed interviews. Participants often cited ways that their perceptions changed about the park and about the dogs being used for service because of the program. Some participants' attitudes appeared to shift after they realized that the dogs were eager to participate on a sled team. Similar perceived attitude change was visible in participants and their understanding about the park, which stemmed from the program.

Empathy

Several participants discussed feelings of empathy towards the dogs and/or rangers that were derived from the one-hour interpretive experience. Feelings regarding the rangers' occupations, respect for the dogs and rangers, as well as respect towards the park and environment were present. Empathy and passion towards the environment and park were seen through various other reflections.

Denali National Park Visitor Center Program

This longitudinal study looked at the recall of visitors who participated in an evening program at Denali National Park. The program focused its subject matter on the premier wildlife of the park: moose, caribou, grizzlies, and Dall sheep. The theme of the program attempted to parallel wildlife and "games" they would play in the wild and children's games. The interpreter was a seasoned veteran who had command of the room within seconds. Her program techniques included "conversation" with the audience, a slide presentation on the animals, storytelling and then an opportunity prior to and following the presentation to touch animal skins and antlers.

Research Design

Thirty-three visitors to the auditorium program held in the summer of 2004 were called approximately one and a half years later, starting in February 2006 to schedule post-program interviews. Of the 33 visitors on the list, 14 were successfully interviewed. Interviews remained unstructured and participant-centered in order to promote participant control of the interview's direction. To analyze the data, the researchers transcribed the interviews and examined each individually through a phenomenological analysis. Clusters of data were organized from the statements; this allowed for the emergence of themes common to all the participants' interviews. Clusters of themes were referred back to the original interview data in order to validate the subjective responses, and a description of the phenomena resulted from the phenomenological analysis.

Results

The most recalled aspects of the program were the props that the interpreter used during the program. In particular, opportunities for visitors and their families to pick up antlers and skins prior to and following the program were much more vivid than content associated with the program. The second emergent recollection was the general recall of the variety of animals the interpreter talked about in the program. These memories were not specific, but they did represent recollections that the program focused on, which relate to animals in the park. The third emergent recollection was the environment of the room, which included the amount of people watching and the warm temperatures of the space. Overall, the most specific recall after 18 months was the action of visitors (or their children) picking up antlers and furs.

Yosemite Valley Tram Tour

This study looked at the recollections of participants of Yosemite National Park's tram tour. During the program, visitors boarded a tram that took them throughout the Yosemite Valley, providing views and information about the many waterfalls found in Yosemite and such well-known geologic formations as El Capitan and Half Dome. Visitors were exposed to the history of the Park Service, park issues, animal and plant information, and current uses of the park, including rock climbing. The tram tour program was about two hours long and included stops along the route for visitors to get off the tram, take photos, and ask the ranger further questions. The tram itself accommodated many visitors and provided a way for visitors to view the valley without having to drive or hike. During the program, the ranger sat in front with a microphone, facing the audience while he or she provided dialogue concerning the things people saw along the way and underlying information. Tour topics included plants and animals, geologic formation of the valley, human history of the park, current uses of the park such as tourism and rock climbing, park stewardship, and issues threatening the park. Four tram tour programs led by four different interpreters over the course of several days in October 2004 were included in the study.

Research Design

A total of 25 telephone interviews of visitors were conducted six months after they attended the tram tour program at Yosemite National Park. Interested visitors were self-selected and provided the principal investigator with their contact information after the tram tour programs at Yosemite. Interview questions were aimed at soliciting from the visitor anything that they recalled from the program and their experiences at Yosemite National Park. The interviews were respondent-led, decreasing the possible bias and impact on responses of the interviewer. All interviews were tape-recorded and transcribed word-for-word. Transcripts were then entered into a computer and analyzed for major emergent themes and subthemes using NVivo qualitative data analysis software. Each interview was first coded using open coding. In open coding, each transcript was analyzed and broken down into short phrases that described any memory a participant had from the program and his or her trip to the park. Using axial coding, the data was organized and analyzed based on emergent themes and patterns. Through axial coding, 12 major themes relating to visitor recollections emerged. Each major theme was further developed with sets of emergent subcategories and subthemes.

Results

For the most part, themes associated with the study were general recollections, with most being broad and not vivid. The most prevalent responses related to two areas: reactions to the rangers and tangible sightings. The theme of ranger attributes included comments regarding the ranger's ability to engage the audience. Twenty-four respondents recalled that the ranger was able to engage his or her audience through a variety of methods and techniques. An overwhelming majority of respondents also described the ranger's attributes in a generally positive manner. These positive comments included the ranger being informative and knowledgeable, being experienced, and having a love for the park and job.

Twenty-three respondents mentioned at least one tangible during their telephone interviews. The main research theme of tangibles included seeing rocks and geological formations, rock climbers, waterfalls, and general views and sights along the tram tour path. Rocks and geological features viewed during the tram tour program were the most frequently recalled tangible aspects, while a majority of the respondents also recalled seeing climbers as a key part of the tram tour program. Twenty visitors recalled, to some degree, viewing the rock climbers during the program.

Hoosier National Forest Campfire Program (Indiana)

This study assessed the impact of an evening interpretive program during July 1999 at the Hoosier National Forest in southern Indiana. This program was a one-hour evening presentation on bats of Indiana. The location of the program was a campground amphitheater. Attendance at the program was approximately 40 people, predominantly in family groups. The general objectives of the presentation were:

- To make visitors aware of the natural history of the bat.
- To make visitors aware of the fallacies of negative bat behavior.
- To improve visitors' attitudes toward bats.

The interpretive program began with a handout "test" that quizzed participants on particular falsehoods regarding bats. Each of the questions was then answered throughout the evening. The statements included items such as, "True or false: Bats have the ability to suck blood from humans." The presentation included a 40-minute slide presentation along with a 15-minute question-and-answer period.

The interpreter, a seasoned naturalist with over 20 years of experience, relied primarily on these two traditional program strategies. There were no hands-on items or other "props."

Research Design
During the fall of 2000 (approximately 14 months following the program), the consenting individuals were contacted by phone and were again asked if they would participate in the study. The semi-structured interviews were organized to accommodate the participants' individual responses and conversation. The interviews began with one general, open-ended question to avoid any cueing of events. Follow-up questions were used with the initial probe to attempt to assure that participant responses were their own thoughts and not statements made to please the interviewer. When the respondent had described her experiences and no further clarification was required, the interview was completed. The length of the interviews varied from 20 to 40 minutes. The raw data was transcribed verbatim for each subject. A phenomenological analysis of the data was conducted:

- All data was read in its entirety by both researchers.
- Significant statements that directly pertained to the phenomenon (participant recall of an interpretive experience) were extracted from each data set.
- Clusters of themes were organized from the statements. This allowed for the emergence of themes common to all the subjects' descriptions.
- These clusters of themes were referred back to the original data in order to validate the data.
- Discrepancies were noted and any inconsistencies were addressed.
- A description of the phenomena resulted from the above results.

Ten people agreed to participate in the study and completed the forms. Out of the original 10 who agreed, only four completed the assessment. All four participants were women ranging in age from mid-20s to late 30s and resided within 30 miles of the Forest Service site. Each had viewed the program with her immediate family (partner and children).

Results
Four themes relating to the participants' recollection of an interpretive program were identified after the interview data was analyzed. The four clusters were novelty, personal significance, speaker qualities, and activities that occur during learning. From what the participants recalled, they tended to remember a part of the program that was novel or unusual, either in the setting or the topic presented. Participants mentioned that they liked or enjoyed the setting being outdoors. They also remembered the pictures of the bats because it was the first opportunity they had to see bats "up close."

The participants recalled some part of the bat program when the information presented was important or relevant to them. These participants were all very concerned about their children's reactions to the program (as mentioned previously, all four participants had children present at the program). They noticed and remembered any part of the program that interested their children. The participants, who are all residents of Indiana, remembered the specific information regarding the Indiana bat, perhaps because they felt the "hometown" species is more important or closely related to them than other species of bats.

Speaker qualities seemed to be another important factor to make the bat program more memorable for the participants in this study. Attributes of the speaker referred to by the participants were very friendly, helpful, very nice, informative, patient, and very good with kids. The speaker's congenial personality made the participants enjoy her presentation and, at the same time, recall the program. Finally, one type of "activity" appeared to facilitate the participants' recollection. The true/false "quiz" given prior to the program was recalled by the participants.

Publication Related to Research
Knapp, D.H., & Yang, L. (2002). A phenomenological analysis of long-term recollections of an interpretive program, *Journal of Interpretation Research,* *7*(2), 7-17.

Brown County State Park Visitor Center Program (Indiana)
The data for this study was gathered from individuals who participated in an evening environmental interpretive program at an Indiana State Park during the fall of 1998. The goals and content of the program dealt with white-tailed deer—a representative mammal in the ecosystem of this region of the country. The general objective and goals of the program were to make visitors aware of the natural history and life patterns of the white-tailed deer. In particular, the program focused on the animals' adaptations for survival and their impact in the region's food web. The program delivery included a 30-minute slide presentation, a 15-minute discussion led by the interpreter, and a "hands-on" period at the end of the program that enabled participants to touch and feel white-tailed deer artifacts. The hour-long program took place inside the park's nature center.

Research Design
Two years following the program, six participants were asked a semi-structured series of open-ended questions that allowed for individual elaboration of rich and meaningful recollection of the program according to the natural flow of conversation. Interviews began with general recall questions to avoid any cueing of responses. Follow-up questions were used within each of these initial probes to assure that participant responses were their own thoughts and not statements made to please the interviewer. Following the interviews, the researchers transcribed the tapes verbatim. Upon reading the transcribed logs, researchers

independently identified and listed statements of meaning, and through a process of mutual negotiation, organized the meaning units into emergent themes.

Results

Four themes emerged from the analysis. Recollections related to: 1) visual cues, 2) novel experiences, 3) interpreter-related actions, and 4) active involvement. The participants remembered visual images related specifically to seeing slides of deer. In the second category of recall, participants noted that aspects of the program were novel or unusual or drew their attention. Antlers and the other touchable items were a consistent response related to this theme. Respondents offered vivid responses related to the interpreter and her style of leading the program and interacting with the audience. The richest description of recalled memories related to active involvement. For example, participants recalled a hearing exercise that involved all of the program participants cupping their ears to demonstrate hearing adaptations of deer. Another active aspect of the program recalled was the passing around of objects that the audience could hold and feel.

Publication Related to Research

Knapp, D.H., & Benton, G. (2005). Long-term recollections of an environmental interpretive program. *Journal of Interpretation Research, 10*(1), 51-55.

School Field Trip Research

Field Trip to George Washington Carver National Monument

This study looked at the long-term impacts of a half-day school field trip to George Washington Carver National Monument. The subjects for this study were members of a fourth-grade class from an elementary school in a rural town near Diamond, Missouri. The multicultural field trip was a half-day, out-of-school experience at the George Washington Carver National Monument conducted in the fall of 2001. During the program, students participated in an interpretive walk on the Carver History Trail and activities conducted at the on-site classroom, science discovery laboratory, and museum and visitor center. The guided walk and indoor activities examined several aspects of Carver's life, including his struggle and success in overcoming the obstacles of slavery, poverty, and poor health and the significant contributions he made to the fields of science and agriculture. The students began with a 45-minute interpretive walk outdoors, then visited three trail sites, including a talking statue of Carver, the Carver house, and the family cemetery. They were then given time to examine the displays in the museum section of the visitor center and were given access to the gift shop. The classroom portion of the program featured rangers informing students about the properties of soybean products and then they participated in an interactive game. The students were then split into two groups, each one alternating between the last two components of the program. One group explored the discovery center with its exhibits, microscopes, and computer terminals, while the other group learned how to make peanut milk and then actually did so in a hands-on activity.

Research Design

A qualitative analysis was conducted on 10 randomly selected students who participated in the formal educational program at the George Washington Carver National Monument. Students who participated in the program were interviewed at least 12 months following the treatment to analyze recollection. Interviews were participant-centered in the sense that participants controlled the direction of the interview, including the subject matter and the range of topics discussed. The responses were transcribed verbatim for each student and a phenomenological analysis was conducted. Each transcript was analyzed and broken down into short phrases that described any memory a participant had from the program and his or her trip to the park. Second, clusters of data were organized from the statements, which allowed for the emergence of themes common to all the subjects' descriptions. These clusters of themes were referred back to the original transcripts in order to validate the responses, and a description of the phenomena resulted from the above analysis.

Results

Two major themes were identified relating to the long-term recollections of the students on the field trip at the George Washington Carver National Monument: 1) recollections were influenced by occasions that incorporated action and involvement, and 2) content information was retained by all students participating in the study.

Student Actions

Participants consistently described their recollection of the park program using action verbs such as "talking, crushing (peanuts), listening, and sitting," and implied action using other words such as "did, went, watched, looked, see, press, showed us." Seven students responded about and described the hands-on activity that conveys Carver's methods and experimentation in the creation of both soy milk and peanut milk. A handful of interpretive displays in the park gained mention by four participants for their active engagement of the visitor.

Educational Content Learning Associated with the Program

Students were descriptive in their recall of this content one year after the experience. George Washington Carver's life and struggles were cited as a learning associated topic by all 10 of the student participants. For example, reflections on a slideshow of Carver's life as a boy were recalled by all participants. Students recalled Carver being displaced from his nuclear family at a young age. Examples of Carver's boyhood life and chores were also discussed by students. Students also recollected information regarding slavery from the program. Students also recalled information about discrimination in public school. Soybeans were the second-most frequently cited learning associated topic, receiving eight citations. These references were associated with products and processes demonstrated in activities and in programs. Tangible aspects of the program were also recalled and aided in retaining information about George Washington Carver. For example, Carver's house received responses from six different participants.

Publications Related to Research

Farmer, J., Knapp, D.H., & Benton, G. (2006). The effects of primary sources and field trip experience on the knowledge retention of multicultural content. *Multicultural Education*, p. 2-6.

Field Trip to Shenandoah National Park

This study evaluated the impact of a science-based field trip to Shenandoah National Park. The subjects for this study were from a fifth-grade class from an elementary school in a rural town in western Virginia. The topics were geologic history and features related to the Shenandoah Valley. The program took place during the fall of 2001 at Loft Mountain located in the southern district of the park. At the base of the mountain the students met park educators and there was a general introduction regarding the day's activities. During the approximately three-hour field trip, students stopped at various locations to discuss general geological information related to the specific site and the region. The first planned experience was a "bag of rocks" activity that had the students look over certain rocks from the area and try to guess each rock's mineral source. Following the bag of rocks activity, the students hiked farther up the mountain to the base of a cliff. At this point, the students were given a clipboard and paper and asked to observe the cliff area for a period of time and write down observations regarding weathering, erosion, and other characteristics of the rock face. At the completion of the debriefing of this second activity, the students completed the hike to the top of the mountain.

Research Design

One year following the out-of-school science program, seven students from the participating fifth-grade class were contacted by phone. These seven were randomly chosen from the list of all 23 students who participated in the program. Interviews were participant centered in the sense that they controlled the direction of the interview, including the subject matter and the range of topics discussed. The raw data was transcribed verbatim for each subject and a phenomenological analysis was conducted. Clusters of themes were organized from the statements, which allowed for the emergence of themes common to all the subjects' descriptions. These clusters of themes were referred back to the original transcripts in order to validate the data.

Results

Two major themes relating to the participants' long-term recollection of the out-of-school science field trip were identified after the interview data was analyzed: 1) recollections were highly influenced by actions taken by the students, and 2) program content and subject matter were retained by all of the students to varying degrees.

Student Actions

Participants described their recollection of the park program using action verbs ending in "ing" (hiking, walking) and also implied action using other words (went, talked, saw, played, sat). All seven respondents used action verbs or nouns to describe student movement in relation to various sites. Six of the seven participants recalled a hands-on lab activity that included identifying rocks from a bag that the park educator provided. The action of seeing and looking was recalled by five of the seven respondents. Particularly, this action statement was associated with the students when given the opportunity to use magnifying glasses to look at rock outcroppings.

Educational Content

All of the participants were able to recall a range of information directly related to the actual educational content that was offered during the out-of-school science field trip. Recall of this information for one year after receiving the content was vivid. Rock knowledge was the most frequently cited learning-associated topic, garnering citations from all seven respondents. Two learning-associated topics (weathering and erosion) received six citations by different participants. The "bag of rocks" activity was also a learning-associated topic, garnering six responses. The responses ranged from general recall to specific content retained from the activity.

Publication Related to Research

Knapp, D.H. (2007). A longitudinal analysis of an out-of-school science experience. *School Science and Mathematics, 107*(2), p. 44-51.

Participation in *Expedition: Yellowstone!* Residential Program

This study evaluated the impact of a residential environmental education program at Yellowstone National Park. The subjects for this study were from a fifth-grade class from an elementary school in a rural town in Idaho. The residential program that these students participated in was titled *Expedition: Yellowstone!* and was conducted in the fall of 2001. This five-day residential program offered students a thorough investigation of the park and its many natural and historical sites.

During the week at *Expedition: Yellowstone!* students experienced a variety of environmental education activities, hikes, and lab investigations. Subjects included geology, water ecology, forest management, and Native American history. The students' housing and meal arrangements were similar to a rustic camp setting. The week-long program based much of its educational strategies on hands-on, interactive experiences.

Research Design

One year following the residential program ten students (10 to 11 years of age) from the same fifth-grade class were contacted by phone. These 10 individuals were randomly chosen from the list of all 33 students who participated in the program. Interviews were participant-centered in the sense that participants controlled the direction of the interview, including the subject matter and the range of topics discussed. The interviewers' responses were limited to minimal encouragement, summaries of content, and clarifications. The responses were transcribed verbatim for each subject and a phenomenological analysis was conducted. All recorded dialogue was read in its entirety by both researchers. Significant statements that directly pertained to the phenomenon (participant recall of the residential environmental education experience) were extracted from each transcript. Clusters of themes were organized from the statements, which allowed for the emergence of themes common to all the subjects' descriptions. These clusters of themes were referred back to the original transcripts in order to validate the responses, and a description of the phenomena resulted from the above analysis.

Results

Three major themes relating to the participants' long-term recollection of the residential environmental education program were identified: 1) recollections were highly influenced by actions taken by the students, 2) program content and subject matter were retained by all of the students to varying degrees, and 3) emotional reactions to the experience were present.

Student Actions

Consistently, participants recalled much of their experience through actions that they had taken during the week at *Expedition: Yellowstone!* All respondents recalled hiking to one or more areas of the park. Game playing was a response from nine of the 10 interviewees. A scavenger hunt and camouflage game were recalled with a great deal of clarity. Another activity that was recalled by eight of the 10 students was journal writing, which was required of the students each day of the week. Another active recollection that gleaned responses from eight of the students was related to an encounter with a bison where the students had to hike off trail and around the animal to avoid a potential incident. Two educational "lab" activities were recalled with some measure of vividness by half of the participants. A landscape erosion activity was described in detail, as was a second field exercise of measuring the chemical make-up of Yellowstone's geysers and surrounding soil.

Program Content

All of the participants were able to recall a range of information directly related to the actual educational content that was offered during the week-long program. Recall of this information for one year after receiving the content was vivid. One feature of Yellowstone that was one of the most recalled topics was the geysers and hot springs. This was related directly to geologic subject matter associated with their visits to these natural phenomena. An analogy (shaking a Coke can) used by the park interpreters during the students' visit at a geyser was clearly recalled 12 months later. Fire ecology, an important subject that was stressed throughout the week, including lessons and field trips to areas of the park that had been damaged by forest fire, was clearly recalled by eight of the students.

Emotional Reactions

Emotional responses related to the students' experiences was the third theme that surfaced from the interview analysis. Much of this emotional category was positive in nature. General enjoyment of the trip was the most frequently cited emotional topic, with nine out of the 10 participants responding positively to one or more experiences related to the residential program. However, there were negative recollections that were also brought up. In particular, residential components of sharing chores, getting up early, and sleeping in the cabins were among the complaints, along with long hikes. Specific activities were also noted by some as negative experiences.

Publications Related to Research

Knapp, D.H., & Benton, G. (2006). Episodic and semantic memories of a residential environmental education program. *Environmental Education Research, 12*(2), 165-177.

Field Trip to Great Smoky Mountains National Park

This study examined the long-term impact of an environmental education school field trip to the Great Smoky Mountains National Park on fourth-grade elementary students during the fall of 2001. The full-day environmental education field trip included a visit to Clingman's Dome (the highest mountain peak in the park), hands-on learning activities, and group discussions led by a ranger from the National Park Service. Students examined spruce and fir trees, discussed the role of the moss spider before the forest ecosystem underwent change, participated in tree identification and food chain activities, hiked a short portion of the Appalachian Trail, partook in an insect and tree discussion, and completed an interactive learning experience using straws, cups, and thumbtacks in order to understand the effect of the woolly adelgid on the Fraser Fir. The rangers then discussed the effect and possible causes of air pollution and led the students through activities at the air-quality monitoring station. Finally, there was a discussion of cars, pollution, environmental impact, and conservation behavior to help address the problem.

Research Design

This study used a phenomenological approach to investigate the impact on the environmental attitude and knowledge of student participants. A qualitative analysis was conducted on 15 randomly selected students who participated in the environmental education program at Great Smoky Mountains National Park. Students who participated in the program were interviewed at least 12 months following the treatment, in order to analyze long-term memory recollection. The responses were transcribed verbatim for each student and a phenomenological analysis was conducted. Each transcript was analyzed and broken down into short phrases that described any memory a participant had from the program and his or her trip to the park. Second, clusters of data were organized from the statements, which allowed for the emergence of themes common to all the subjects' descriptions.

Results

Three major themes were identified relating to the long-term recollections of the students on the environmental education field trip at Great Smoky Mountains National Park: 1) recollections were influenced by occasions that incorporated action and involvement, 2) content information was retained by a vast majority of students, and 3) ecological knowledge and environmental attitude were displayed by many study participants one year after the field trip.

Student Actions

Participants consistently described their recollection of the park program using action verbs such as walking, hiking, seeing, drawing, and talking and implied action utilizing other words such as "did, went played, showed us, and measured." All 15 students used action words or phrases to describe the events of the field trip experience. Terms such as *identifying* (leaf-tree), *drawing and tracing, studying and learning, memorizing, sucking* (straws), *poking holes, sipping, learned about* (bugs), *touch them, heard* (bugs), *monitoring, measuring* (air and wind speed), *charting air pollution, graphing, working on project, did project/activity*, and *doing activity* were used to describe events encountered on the field trip. Thirteen of the 15 students used action terms to describe the walking, hiking, and climbing aspects of the environmental education program. Ten of the 15 students shared memories of actions related to the ranger-led program.

Educational Content and Learning Associated with the Program
The educational content and learning association category represents three distinct components: program information, knowledge gained, and learning derived from educational activities. Students were descriptive in their recall of this content one year after the experience. For example, the activity of using the straw and cup was cited as a learning associated topic by 10 of the 15 student participants. The pollution monitoring activity, in which students graphed the change in air pollution, was cited by nine students.

Ecological and Environmental Attitude of Program Participants
The ecological and environmental theme can be categorized into two separate subthemes: ecological knowledge and pro-environmental attitude. Fourteen of the 15 student participants recalled details representing ecological or environmental knowledge. Participants consistently described their recollection of the park program using ecological principles and terminology such as *bugs kill trees, deprives tree of nutrients, attracted to chemicals, parasite, invasive species, transferred from exotic country, non-native tree-accident, trying to kill bug, pellet to kill, pesticide, lifecycle,* and *food chain*. Twelve of the 15 students used words or phrases correlating to the woolly adelgid (the exotic species responsible for the degradation of the spruce and fir trees), possible tools used to halt the invasive insect, and usefulness of the trees for human consumption.

Publications Related to Research
Farmer, J., Knapp, D., & Benton, G. (2007). A qualitative analysis of the long-term impact of an elementary environmental education field trip on ecological/ environmental knowledge and attitude development. *Journal of Environmental Education, 38*(4).

Field Trip to Thomson Park (Bloomington, Indiana)
Third and fourth graders took an environmental science field trip during the spring of 1996. The program's site was a city park and preserve approximately five miles from the participating schools. The field trip followed a script that was divided into seven sections: 1) during the introductory section, the field teacher set standards and goals for the day, conducted an introductory game or activity, and set up a plant transpiration experiment; 2) the discovery section allowed students to collect plants (in a scavenger hunt format), ask questions, and discuss aspects of the vegetation found; 3) during the discussion section, a plant adaptation activity was conducted and students were guided through discussions on adaptation, the importance of plants, and plant facts; 4) a guided hike allowed students to discover plant adaptations and to discuss adaptations and their functions; 5) after the walk, the transpiration experiment was discussed; 6) the field teacher then asked a series of review questions; and 7) the students

participated in a concluding game or activity. Subjects were 71 third- and fourth-grade students from a rural, Midwestern elementary school.

Research Design

The survey instrument consisted of four open-ended questions and was completed by most respondents in less than 15 minutes. The instrument used a cued recall and a funneled approach so that the earlier questions would not prompt memories relevant to subsequent questions. The survey was administered one month and 18 months after the completion of the field trip. After the data from the one-month post-survey was collected, two researchers coded the data into categories for content analysis. The two sets of independently generated categories agreed highly and additional discussions created a set of agreed-upon groupings. These same groupings were used in the subsequent analysis of the data collected at 18 months. The high level of agreement between researchers working independently supports the validity of the emergent categories generated.

Results

The results from both the one-month and 18-month post-tests yielded similar categories of answer responses. Both post-tests administered during this study revealed that memories were nonspecific and disassociated from specific information given by the field teacher. In fact, most of the participants during the test could not recall the specific activity that was used to associate transpiration—a concept reviewed during the field trip. However, results yielded positive responses to returning to the field trip site. This implies that while not retaining specific objective-oriented content, students did gain a positive reaction to returning to the park that continued over the long term. While very few of the surveys contained specific references to what was learned about plants, many contained references to the introductory song and games that were played. Responses included, "the treasure hunt we did" or "doing the taped thumb game." This supports the idea that activities that involve multiple sensations are more memorable. It is likely that these games and songs were both novel and emotionally charged, which would make them more memorable.

Publications Related to Research

Knapp, D.H. (2000). Memorable experiences of a science field trip. *School Science and Mathematics, 100*(2), 65-72.

Field Trips to Hoosier National Forest (Indiana)

This study assessed the impact on students participating in a field trip to a U.S. Forest Service site near their school district during the fall of 1998. The interpretive experience was conducted at the Charles Deam Wilderness located in the Hoosier National Forest. Participants of this study were 24 fourth graders from three classes from a rural town in southern Indiana. The goals of the program were to:

- Make students aware of the rules and regulations of a wilderness site.
- Enable students to explore the site in an experiential nature.
- Make students aware of environmental issues associated with the Deam Wilderness.
- Make students aware of basic ecological concepts.

Methodologies utilized in this program included ranger-led discussions, exploratory hiking, facilitated explorations, and nature games.

Research Design

This study involved a discursive approach to emergent design to generate a grounded theory. The phenomenological data gathered during the research directed the design of each step of the study as it evolved. The categories, themes, hypothesis, and subsequent theory that emerged were grounded in the data. This study began with an assessment of students' knowledge and attitudes about the resource site one week before their interpretive experience. Questions were posed to the students to probe any previous experiences at the resource site they were about to visit. They were also asked what they may learn and discover during their trip, as well as what they may enjoy the most during their coming experience. Finally, a question was posed to the students to learn if they believed their participation in the interpretive program would change the way they would act toward the site after the event.

Post-interviews were conducted one week following the experience, and post-post-interviews were conducted four months later. The questioning technique was open-ended, with the participant leading the discussion as much as possible. Follow-up questions were used with each of these initial probes to attempt to assure that their responses were their own thoughts and not statements made to please the interviewer. Following the interviews, the researchers transcribed the tapes in the form of a log resembling field notes, which is associated with ethnographic research. After reading the log material the researchers applied a set of substantive codes to the entries by categorizing the observational, theoretical, and methodological notes.

Results

An emerging theme that came from the analysis of the categories was that student actions formed the basis for recollection of the interpretive program and those actions were important in influencing knowledge and attitude. An experience that had students catching, looking, searching, chasing, acting, etc., was more successful in its retention than aspects that were didactic and passive. The predominant actions of the students occurred in conjunction with the exploratory activities and games that the interpreter offered during the program. Students had vivid accounts of these experiences—in particular, the mechanics of the activities and their roles in these games. Virtually all participants looked upon the field trip as a positive experience. This positive outlook was transferred to the resource site.

Passive experiences associated with the interpretive program had an opposite impact. Cognitive information such as ecological concepts, wilderness information, and environmental issue information was vaguely recalled at best and in many cases misunderstood or misinterpreted. Unless information was directly imbedded in the games, students found it difficult to recall any specific information four months after the field trip. The willingness on the part of the student to act on issues associated with the resource site was negligible. Students were disinterested in taking personal actions to improve or help solve an environmental issue related to the wilderness.

Publication Related to Research
Knapp, D.H., & Poff, R. (2001). A qualitative analysis of the immediate and short-term impact of an interpretive program. *Environmental Education Research,* *7*(1), 55-65.

South Central Indiana Environmental Education Partnership Project

This multi-year project offered partnerships between middle schools in southcentral Indiana and the Hoosier National Forest from 1994 to 1995. A five-phase curriculum that represented all of the major variables associated with environmental behavior change (see Chapter 4) was offered to participating classes. Below is a description of each of the five phases of the project:

Phase 1: Basic Knowledge of Wilderness Site:
   Students learned basic ecological principles regarding southcentral Indiana ecosystems, as well as the natural and cultural history of the Deam Wilderness.

Phase 2: Awareness of Problems and Issues Associated with Site:
   Students learned about the problems and issues associated with the Deam Wilderness by analyzing some wilderness site issues and examining certain wilderness problems.

Phase 3: Investigation of Wilderness Site Issues:
   Strategies and methods were taught with respect to collecting data and summarizing results. Students developed surveys and performed class research projects during this period.

Phase 4: Knowledge of Citizen Participation Skills:
   Students were taught methods of communicating their results in a public

setting. In addition, students were taught different action skills related to responsible environmental behavior.

Phase 5: Wilderness Summit:

All of the participating students met with the U.S. Forest Service officials to report recommendations regarding management of the Deam Wilderness. These recommendations were a result of their surveys and research completed between Phases 3 and 4.

Several training sessions were held to prepare the teachers and interpreters for the pre- and post-activities and field trip lessons and to develop guidelines for the student research projects. An assembly was held each year after the interpretive experiences, where the student research projects were reviewed. At this meeting, the students were able to showcase their efforts in front of peers, instructors, and Forest Service officials. The event's format allowed Forest Service officials to respond to comments and questions generated during the student presentations. The population the first year was 120 seventh- and eighth-grade students from three different middle schools; 71 eighth-grade students were assessed during the second year.

Research Design

First Year: A 15-item questionnaire was developed to measure students' knowledge, attitudes, and behaviors with respect to each of the interpretive phases of the project. The instrument was administered before and after each of the interpretive experiences, as well as before the start of the program. An independent samples T-test was used to analyze the data from the completed surveys. A second component of analysis was interviews with participating teachers. Comments during the first two phases were generally positive, while comments during the third and fourth phases of the program were mixed. First, teachers felt the investment on the part of the students was a valuable component to developing a positive attitude and behavior with respect to the wilderness. However, they did feel that the research projects took a great deal of time out of their already busy schedule.

Second Year: A revised 20-item questionnaire was developed to measure the second year's program on students' knowledge, attitude, and behavior toward the wilderness. The instrument was administered before and after each of the interpretive experiences, as well as before the start of the program. Researchers used a T-test: Paired Two-Sample for Means to determine any changes in the three variables. The second component, again, was interviews with participating teachers. Comments during the first two phases were similar to those from the first year. They generally conveyed a positive attitude toward the field trips. They also believed that the information on the issues of the Deam Wilderness was quite helpful. However, they found the project to be a challenge in regard to the time commitment for both teacher preparation and student involvement.

Results

Of the three variables (knowledge, attitude, and behavior), only the knowledge questions showed a significant increase throughout the program. The greatest increase in knowledge took place during the first phase of the program in which students were taught basic ecological principles, as well as the natural and cultural history of the Deam Wilderness. Alternatively, the attitude and behavior variables did not reflect a significant change throughout the program.

Publication Related to Research

Marsan, S., & Knapp, D.H. (1996). The Deam Wilderness interpretive program. *Interpedge, 3*(3), 20-25.

Knapp, D.H. (1997). Back to the basics: Interpreting to the lowest common denominator. *Trends: Interpretation as Communication, 34*(4), 17-21.

School Field Trips to Indiana Dunes National Lakeshore

This study evaluated the impact of two different interpretive experiences on elementary students' environmental knowledge, attitude, and behavior. Each program represented a major variable associated with the attitude and behavior change goals supported by interpreters. These programs were administered and evaluated during the 1995–1996 school year at the Paul H. Douglas Environmental Education Center at Indiana Dunes National Lakeshore. Approximately 1,500 students participated in both programs, representing 705 fourth graders, 637 fifth graders, and 213 sixth graders. The first interpretive experience, offered during the fall, was dedicated to ecological information while the second program was conducted in the spring and was based on environmental issues associated with the site.

The ecology program, designed and presented by interpretive rangers at Indiana Dunes National Lakeshore, included student participation in investigating differences among habitats encountered on a guided walk. The "Habitats Hike" enforced the theme that the variety of habitats at Indiana Dunes National Lakeshore support an abundance of animal and plant life, while each of these habitats contains a mixture of different conditions under which certain plants and animals can survive. At the end of the program, it was expected that students would be able to describe how light, moisture, and temperature differ in four different habitats, and how this determines which animals and plants live in each of these habitats. In addition, students would be able to describe the common plants of each habitat, explain which signs of animals they found in each habitat, and explain why species diversity is important in nature.

The second treatment was based on environmental issues associated with the national lakeshore. The program "A Grain of Truth" was designed to introduce the theme that the dunes at the national lakeshore are a dynamic place formed by the actions of glaciers, wind, and plants. At the end of the program, students should have been able to understand how and why humans impact the dunes and realize the influence humans have on the succession process of a dune ecosystem. A variety of other environmental issues were conveyed to the students during the interpretive hike.

Research Design

To evaluate the impact the programs had on students' knowledge and attitudes toward the environment, a quasi-experimental design was implemented using an evaluation instrument that included 15 multiple-choice questions. The validity of this evaluation was established by a critique jury made up of Indiana Dunes interpreters who observed that the instrument reflected information and attitudes desired following an environmental science field trip. Participating teachers administered the evaluation instrument one to two days prior to each treatment (the pre-test) and immediately after the class attended the programs (the post-test). The evaluation instrument remained the same throughout the fall and spring sessions. All tests in the study were given in the classroom and then sent to Indiana University for analysis. The evaluation instrument consisted of three sections: knowledge, attitude, and behavior intent. Five multiple-choice questions evaluated the retention of key ecological concepts that were discussed during both field trips. The second set of multiple-choice questions measured potential attitude change regarding the resource site. The final questions determined if positive environmental behavior increased following the field trip.

Multiple analysis of variance was used to evaluate the knowledge and attitude sections of the instrument. The independent variable of the order in which the treatments were received was treated as an independent measure. The independent variable of when students took the test (before the program or after the program) was a repeated measure. The study randomly assigned the order the classes received the treatments. Data was analyzed using the MANOVA command in SPSS 7.5.

Results

The results of this study showed significant gains in science-related knowledge following both the ecology and issue-oriented treatments. The data indicates that the focus of the program (ecology or issues) did not significantly alter the way students responded to the knowledge section of the evaluation instrument. This suggests that both ecology-centered and issue-oriented programs are effective at influencing student knowledge gain. A second conclusion from this study is that there did seem to be an additive effect with regards to ecological and issue knowledge. Students had a high rate of retention of program information prior to the second treatment, which rose further following this program. Results regarding the impact on attitude and behavior were mixed. Analysis of differences from the pre-test to the post-test for both ecology- and issue-oriented programs did not show significant differences in attitudes and behavior. The results did not support the notion that either a science-content program or an issue-laden message could improve the attitudes of the students. Neither the natural history hike nor the issue investigation program raised the students' interest to return to the site.

Publications Related to Research

Knapp, D.H., & Barrie, E. (2001). Content evaluation of an environmental science field trip. *Journal of Science Education and Technology, 10*(4), 351-357.

Knapp, D.H. (2001). Content analysis of interpretive restoration programs. *Ecological Restoration, 19*(1), 58-60.

Knapp, D.H., & Barrie, E. (1999). Ecology versus issue interpretation: The analysis of two different messages. *Journal of Interpretation Research, 3*(1), 21-38.

Three Year Post Analysis of a Field Trip to Hilltop Nature Center (Bloomington, Indiana)

During the spring of 1995, one third-grade class (20 students) from southcentral Indiana participated in a field trip to the Hilltop Garden and Nature Center. This interpretive program, which lasted for a half day, was led by an environmental education specialist. The subject matter contained in the interpretive experience focused on animal adaptations. Several lessons were conducted along with games from the Project Wild curriculum. Three years later, students were contacted and interviewed to learn what recollections they had of the field trip.

Research Design

Ten sixth-grade students who had participated in the field trip during the third grade were contacted three years later. They were interviewed and asked to recall the experience they had at Hilltop. Due to the longitudinal nature of this study, the researchers made sure questions and responses were associated with that specific experience. Answers were transcribed verbatim for each student and analysis was conducted. Each transcript was analyzed and broken down into short phrases that described any memory a participant had from the program and his or her experience at Hilltop. Second, clusters of data were organized from the statements, which allowed for the emergence of themes common to all the subjects' descriptions.

Results

Responses were very general or nondescript due to the length of time between the interpretive program and contact with the participants. No specific content was retained, although some recalled they were there to learn about plants and animals. The one specific aspect of the program that was recalled in some detail was a Project Wild game that pertained to the difficulty in bird migration. Students remembered both the game mechanics and the content associated with the game. The other consistent finding was the positive affect toward the visit and the facility.

Publication Related to Research

Sibthorp, J., & Knapp, D.H. (1998). Evaluating short-term and long-term retention experiences associated with an interpretive school field trip. *Coalition for Education in the Outdoors: Fourth Research Symposium Proceedings* [Refereed]. Cortland, NY: Coalition for Education in the Outdoors, pp. 92-103.

Field Trips to Hilltop Garden and Nature Center (Bloomington, Indiana)

During the fall and spring of 1993 and 1994, approximately 30 third and fourth-grade classes (600 students) from southcentral Indiana participated in conservation and environmental activities at the Hilltop Garden and Nature Center. Through a series of meetings with participating school teachers and agency officials, an interpretive program was developed that answered the needs of the teachers' class curricula. The actual experiences and activities used in these programs were taken from existing environmental and conservation resources such as Project Learning Tree, Project Wild, and OBIS (Outdoor Biological Instructional Strategies). The subject matter contained in the interpretive experience focused on plant adaptations. This was an important science concept that both the third- and fourth-grade students were learning through the Science Curriculum Improvement Study (SCIS). These interpretive programs, which lasted for a half day, were led by an environmental education specialist.

Research Design

A quasi-experimental design was used to conduct this research. A pre-test was administered to students prior to any pre-field trip lessons. A pre-visit test was given before their visit to the Hilltop facility and a post-test was administered to students at the school following the experience. These evaluations, which were approved by the teachers, measured any knowledge and/or attitude change that resulted from students' participation in the interpretation program at Hilltop. The result of each question was analyzed to learn if any attitude or knowledge change occurred during or following the interpretive experience. This was accomplished through conducting chi-square tests to determine if there was a relationship between the students' answers and the time they took the test. In order to determine if the terms used while teaching the students about plants had an effect on their answers, another chi-square was run for independence. This test divided the responses into two categories: those who responded in terms used during the interpretive program and those not used. F-tests were also run to determine if there were any significant changes in scores.

Results

The results of this quasi-experimental design show significant changes in students' knowledge of plant adaptations after their interpretive experience. All knowledge-related questions showed some significance in scores following the Hilltop program. However, the attitude-related questions showed no significant difference. This data supports the notion that an interpretive experience can aid a student's awareness in science or ecological subject matter. It does not support the notion that such a short experience can affect a student's attitude toward that subject matter.

Publications Related to Research
Drake, T., & Knapp, D.H. (1994). The Hilltop Interpretation project. *The Interpretive Sourcebook: Proceedings of the 1994 National Interpreters Workshop* [Refereed]. Madison, WI: Omnipress, pp. 282-292.

Model Development Research

The Development of a Model of Learning for Interpretation
This work was an attempt to develop a model of learning related to interpretation based on long-term memory. Following 15 years of research, studies' results consistently offered visitor impact more associated with recall and retention than behavior or attitude change.

Research Design
The first phase of this work was the review of literature in cognitive sciences related to long-term memory and its application through episodic events such as an interpretive program. This process dealt with work from Endel Tulving dealing with episodic and semantic memory. In relationship to interpretation, episodic memory allows individuals to recall the actual interpretive program and topic(s) and other specific information related to the event. Semantic memory enables the individual to draw in general knowledge that could be stimulated by the episodic memory. Hypothetically, information attached to the episodic recollection would assimilate into the more conceptual semantic knowledge. This theory was then developed as a learning model for interpretation. This model is couched in episodic and semantic memory systems. The model is based on the idea that an interpretive event would offer a set of experiences that would relate to one or more of the three variables that enhance episodic memory systems (active experiences, repetitive content, and information relative to the participants).

Results
Results from several of the studies conducted by the author and discussed in the book support two of the three variables of the learning model. Both active experiences and relevant information have been found consistently to create long-term recollection for participants of an interpretive program. The third variable, repetitive content, implies long-term experiences and therefore would not relate to this model. Also, the breadth and depth of recall related to a variety of the research

suggests the development of semantic memories, which can attribute to conceptual knowledge.

Publications Related to Research
Knapp, D.H. (2006). The development of semantic memories through interpretation. *Journal of Interpretation Research, 11*(2), p. 21-35.
Knapp, D.H., & Benton, G. (2006). Episodic and semantic memories of a residential environmental education program. *Environmental Education Research, 12*(2), 165-177.

Development of an Environmental Interpretation Behavior Change Model

The purpose of this study was to produce a broad framework of goals for environmental interpretation and to revise and validate these goals based on input from a national panel of interpretive experts. Several tasks were accomplished in an attempt to complete these goals. First, an intensive review of interpretive literature that produced over 100 principles, goals, and objectives in interpretation was conducted. An analysis of the key words and phrases utilized in these principles, goals, and objectives yielded categories of directives for environmental interpretation. A review of research studies related to environmental behavior paradigms was then conducted. Following this review, the Hungerford & Volk (1990) model of variables involved in responsible environmental behavior was utilized as the basis for a framework for environmental interpretation goals related to behavior change. This integration produced an initial set of Goals for Program Development in Environmental Interpretation.

Research Design
An instrument was developed to evaluate the Goals for Program Development in Environmental Interpretation. The instrument used a yes/no response to avoid neutral comments that a Likert scale measurement could have produced. Leaders in the field of interpretation were identified as potential members of the validity panel that would complete the instrument. This selection included authors of published principles, goals, and/or objectives in interpretation who were assumed to have had experience or expertise in the field of interpretation. The resulting validity panel consisted of 18 leaders in interpretation. The evaluation instrument and program goals were sent to each panelist. Of the 18 panel members contacted and sent instruments, 15 evaluations were returned. Thirteen of these were completed or partially completed, yielding a return rate of 72 percent. Following the return of the completed evaluations, a synthesis of responses was conducted.

Results
The results of this analysis were then integrated into the program development goals. The analysis of the evaluation conducted by the panel of experts supported the validation of the Goals for Program Development in Environmental

Interpretation. The majority of the experts believed that the program goals represented important outcomes for environmental interpretive programs. They also believed that these goals are important in effecting knowledge, attitude, and/or behavior change in a resource site visitor. The response to each goal received a range of 62 to 100 percent approval rate. No goal received less than a two-to-one majority of the respondent approval.

Publication Related to Research

Knapp, D.H., Volk T.L., & Hungerford, H.R. (1997). Producing empirically derived goals for program development in environmental interpretation. *Journal of Environmental Education 28*(3), 24-35.

Knapp, D.H. (1995). Moving beyond Tilden: Producing behavior change goals for environmental interpretation. *Legacy: Journal of the National Association for Interpretation, 6*(1), 24-27.

Appendix: References

Chapter References

Chapter 1

Conway, M. A., Perfect, T. J., Anderson, S. J., Gardiner, J. M., & Cohen, G. M. (1997). Changes in memory awareness during learning: The acquisition of knowledge by psychology undergraduates. *Journal of Experimental Psychology, 126*(4), 393-413.

Herbert, D. M., & Burt, J. S. (2004). What do students remember? Episodic memory and the development of schematization. *Applied Cognitive Psychology, 18,* 77-88.

Knapp, D.H., & Barrie, E. (2001). Content evaluation of an environmental science field trip. *Journal of Science Education and Technology, 10*(4), 351-357.

Koriat, A. (2003). Memory organization of action events and its relationship to memory performance. *Journal of Experimental Psychology, 132*(3), 435-454.

Ramsden, P. (1997). The context of learning. In F. Martin, D. Hounsell, & N. Entwistle (Eds), *The experience of learning: Implications for teaching and studying in higher education.* Edinburgh: Scottish Academic Press.

Semb, G. B., & Ellis, J. A. (1994). Knowledge taught in school: What is remembered? *Review of Educational Research, 64,* 253-286.

Tilden, F. (1957). *Interpreting our heritage.* Chapel Hill, NC: University of North Carolina.

Tulving, E. (1972). Episodic and semantic memory. In E. Tulving and W. Donaldson (Eds.), *Organization of memory* (381-403). New York: Academic Press.

Tulving, E. (1983). *Elements of episodic memory.* New York: Oxford University Press.

Chapter 2

Brochu, L., & Merriman, T. (2001). *Certified interpretive guide training book.* Ft. Collins, CO: National Association for Interpretation.

Ham, S. (1992). *Environmental interpretation: A practical guide for people with big ideas and small budgets.* Golden, CO: North American Press.

Larsen, D. (Ed.). (2003). *Meaningful interpretation: How to connect hearts and minds to places, objects, and other resources.* Ft. Washington, PA: Eastern National.

Larsen, D. L. (2002). Be relevant or become a relic. *Journal of Interpretation Research, 7*(1), 17-23.

Mackintosh, B. (1986). *Interpretation in the National Park Service.* Washington D.C.: National Park Service.

Tilden, F. (1957). *Interpreting our heritage.* Chapel Hill, NC: University of North Carolina.

Chapter 3

Mackintosh, B. (1986). *Interpretation in the National Park Service.* Washington D.C.: National Park Service.

National Park Service (1938). *Recreational use of land in the United States.* Published report on land planning. Washington D.C.: National Park Service.

Chapter 4

Ballantyne, R., & Uzzell, D. (1993). Environmental mediation and hot interpretation: A case study of District Six, Cape Town. *Journal of Environmental Education, 24*(3), 4-7.

Brown, W. E. (1971). *Islands of hope.* Arlington, VA: National Recreation and Park Association.

Chawla, L. (1998). Research methods to investigate significant life experiences: Review and recommendations. *Environmental Education Research, 4,* 383-398.

Drake, T., & Knapp, D.H. (1994). The Hilltop interpretation project. *The Interpretive Sourcebook: Proceedings of the 1994 National Interpreters Workshop* [Refereed]. Madison, WI: Omnipress, pp. 282-292.

Ham, S.H., & Krumpe, E.E. (1996). Identifying audiences and messages for nonformal environmental education: A theoretical framework for interpreters. *Journal of Interpretation Research, 1*(1), 11-23.

Hungerford, H. R., & Volk, T. L. (1990). Changing learner behavior through environmental education. *Journal of Environmental Education, 21*(3), 8-21.

Hungerford, H., Peyton, R. B., and Wilke, R. J., (1980). Goals for curriculum development in environmental education. *Journal of Environmental Education, 11*(3), 42-46.

Isaac, S., & Michael, W. B. (1990). *Handbook in research and evaluation.* San Diego, CA: Edits.

Knapp, D.H., & Barrie, E. (1999). Ecology versus issue interpretation: The analysis of two different messages. *Journal of Interpretation Research, 3*(1), 21-38.

Knapp, D.H., Volk T.L., & Hungerford, H.R. (1997). Producing empirically derived goals for program development in environmental interpretation. *Journal of Environmental Education, 28*(3), 24-35.

Louv, R. (2005). *Last child in the woods.* New York: Workman Publishing.

Mackintosh, B. (1986). *Interpretation in the National Park Service.* Washington D.C.: National Park Service.

Marsan, S., & Knapp, D.H. (1996). The Deam Wilderness interpretive program. *Interpedge, 3*(3), 20-25.

Nash, R. (1991). The rights of nature and the frontiers of interpretation. *Proceedings: 1991 National Interpreters Workshop*, Preface.

National Park Service. (1991). *National park education task force: A report and recommendations.* Washington D.C.

National Park Service. (2007). http://www.nps.gov/idp/interp.

Sharpe, G. (1982). *Interpreting the environment.* New York: Wiley & Sons.

Sobel, D. (1999). *Beyond ecophobia: Reclaiming the heart in nature education.* Barrington, MA: Orion Society.

Tanner, T. (1998). Forward to special issue. *Environmental Education Research, 4*(4), p. 365.

Tilden, F. (1957). *Interpreting our heritage.* Chapel Hill, NC: University of North Carolina.

Vander Stoep, G. A. (1995). Trends in interpretation. In: *Proceedings of the Fourth International Outdoor Recreation & Tourism Trends Symposium.* St. Paul: University of Minnesota: 467-472.

Weilbacher, M. (1994). Eight for the earth. *E Magazine*, December, 28.

Chapter 5
California State Parks. (2003). *Roving: Basic interpretation handbook.* Unpublished document.

Chapter 6
Orion, N. (1993). A model for the development and implementation of field trips as an integral part of the science curriculum. *School Science and Mathematics, 93*(6), p. 325-331.

Trowbridge, L. W., & Bybee, R. W. (1990). *Becoming a secondary school science teacher.* New York: Merrill.

Chapter 7
Abbey, E. (1990). *Desert solitaire.* New York: Touchstone.

Eisenberger, R. & Loomis, R.J. (2003). Visitor experience and media effectiveness: Rocky Mountain and Yellowstone National Parks. Unpublished research report.

Forist, B. E. (2003). *Visitor use and evaluation of interpretive media.* Technical research report, Washington D.C.: National Park Service.

George Washington Carver National Monument. (2001). *General management plan.* Unpublished park document.

Vaughn, S. (2004). It's a matter of balance. *Journal of Interpretation Research, 9*(2), p. 61-64.

Yellowstone National Park. (2001). *Expedition: Yellowstone! management plan.* Unpublished park document.

Chapter 8

Knapp, D.H., & Poff, R. (2001). A qualitative analysis of the immediate and short-term impact of an interpretive program. *Environmental Education Research, 7*(1), 55-65.

Tilden, F. (1957). *Interpreting our heritage.* Chapel Hill, NC: University of North Carolina.

Research References

Refereed Journal Articles

Farmer, J., Knapp, D., & Benton, G. (2007). A qualitative analysis of the long-term impact of an elementary environmental education field trip on ecological/environmental knowledge and attitude development. *Journal of Environmental Education, 38*(4).

Knapp, D.H. (2007). A longitudinal analysis of an out-of-school science experience. *School Science and Mathematics, 107*(2), p. 44-51.

Knapp, D.H. (2006). The development of semantic memories through interpretation. *Journal of Interpretation Research, 11*(2), p. 21-35.

Knapp, D.H., & Benton, G. (2006). Episodic and semantic memories of a residential environmental education program. *Environmental Education Research, 12*(2), 165-177.

Farmer, J, Knapp, D.H., & Benton, G. (2006). The effects of primary sources and field trip experience on the knowledge retention of multicultural content. *Multicultural Education*, p. 2-6.

Knapp, D.H., & Benton, G. (2005). Long-term recollections of an environmental interpretive program. *Journal of Interpretation Research, 10*(1), 51-55.

Knapp, D.H., & Benton, G. (2004). Analysis of interpretive programs at selected National Park Service units: Variables for successful interpretation. *Journal of Interpretation Research, 9*(2), 9-25.

Knapp, D.H., & Yang, L. (2002). A phenomenological analysis of long term recollections of an interpretive program. *Journal of Interpretation Research, 7*(2), 7-17.

Knapp, D.H., & Barrie, E. (2001). Content evaluation of an environmental science field trip. *Journal of Science Education and Technology, 10*(4), 351-357.

Knapp, D.H. (2001). Content analysis of interpretive restoration programs. *Ecological Restoration, 19*(1), 58-60.

Knapp, D.H., & Poff, R. (2001). A qualitative analysis of the immediate and short-term impact of an interpretive program. *Environmental Education Research, 7*(1), 55-65.

Knapp, D.H. (2000). Memorable experiences of a science field trip. *School Science and Mathematics, 100*(2), 65-72.

Knapp, D.H. (2000). The Thessaloniki declaration: A wake-up call for environmental education? *Journal of Environmental Education, 31*(3), 32-39.

Knapp, D.H., & Barrie, E. (1999). Ecology versus issue interpretation: The analysis of two different messages. *Journal of Interpretation Research, 3*(1), 21-38.

Sibthorp, J., & Knapp, D.H. (1998). Evaluating short-term and long-term retention experiences associated with an interpretive school field trip. *Coalition for Education in the Outdoors: Fourth Research Symposium Proceedings* [Refereed]. Cortland, NY: Coalition for Education in the Outdoors, pp. 92-103.

Knapp, D.H., Volk T.L., & Hungerford, H.R. (1997). Producing empirically derived goals for program development in environmental interpretation. *Journal of Environmental Education, 28*(3), 24-35.

Knapp, D.H. (1996). Evaluating the impact of environmental interpretation: A review of three research studies. *Coalition for Education in the Outdoors: Third Research Symposium Proceedings* [Refereed]. Cortland, NY: Coalition for Education in the Outdoors, pp. 127-136.

Knapp, D.H., & Barrie, E. (1995). Should we interpret issues or ecology? *The Interpretive Sourcebook: Proceedings of the 1995 National Interpreters' Workshop* [Refereed]. Madison, WI: Omnipress, pp. 330-345.

Knapp, D.H. (1995). Moving beyond Tilden: Producing behavior change goals for environmental interpretation. *Legacy: Journal of the National Association for Interpretation, 6*(1), 24-27.

Drake, T., & Knapp, D.H. (1994). The Hilltop interpretation project. *The Interpretive Sourcebook: Proceedings of the 1994 National Interpreters Workshop* [Refereed]. Madison, WI: Omnipress, pp. 282-292.

Professional Publications

Knapp, D.H. (2005). The case for a constructivist approach to interpretation. *The Interpreter.* Fort Collins, CO: National Association for Interpretation.

Knapp, D.H. (2003). Interpretation that works. *Legacy: The Magazine of the National Association for Interpretation, 14*(6), 26-33.

Knapp, D.H., & Marsan, S. (1998). Solving wilderness issues: An environmental education partnership that involves students in wilderness management. *Wilderness and Natural Areas in Eastern North America: Research, Management and Planning.* Nacogdoches, TX: Stephen F. Austin University.

Knapp, D.H. (1997). Back to the basics: Interpreting to the lowest common denominator. *Trends: Interpretation as Communication, 34*(4), 17-21.

Knapp, D.H. (1997). The relationship between environmental interpretation and environmental education. *Legacy: The Magazine of the National Association for Interpretation, 8*(3) 10-13.

Marsan, S., & Knapp, D.H. (1996). The Deam Wilderness interpretive program. *Interpedge, 3*(3), 20-25.

Knapp, D.H., & Barrie, E. (1996). Sand dunes vs. Earth Day issues: Comparing impacts of issues and ecology programming on audiences. *Interpscan: Interpretation Canada, 23*(2), 13-16.

Wadzinski, L., & Knapp, D.H. (1995). Saving an "unwild" wilderness through interpretation. *Legacy: The Journal of the National Association for Interpretation, 6*(6), 20-22.

Technical Research Reports

Knapp, D.H., & Benton, G. (2004). *Analysis of Interpretive Programs at Selected National Park Service Units: Phase II Research Report: Yellowstone National Park*. National Park Service: Washington D.C.

Knapp, D.H., & Benton, G. (2004). *Analysis of Interpretive Programs at Selected National Park Service Units: Phase II Research Report: Shenandoah National Park*. National Park Service: Washington D.C.

Knapp, D.H., & Benton, G. (2004). *Analysis of Interpretive Programs at Selected National Park Service Units: Phase II Research Report: Great Smoky Mountains National Park*. National Park Service: Washington D.C.

Knapp, D.H., & Benton, G. (2004). *Analysis of Interpretive Programs at Selected National Park Service Units: Phase II Research Report: George Washington Carver National Monument*. National Park Service: Washington D.C.

Knapp, D.H. (2003). *Variables for Successful Interpretation: Analysis of Interpretive Programs at Selected National Park Service Units*. National Park Service: Washington D.C.

Knapp, D.H., & Benton, G. (2003). *Case Study Analysis of George Washington Carver National Monument*. National Park Service: Washington D.C.

Knapp, D.H. & Monimee, G. (2003). *Case Study Analysis of Shenandoah National Park*. National Park Service: Washington D.C.

Knapp, D. H. & Bareford, K. (2003). *Case Study Analysis of Yellowstone National Park*. National Park Service: Washington D.C.

Knapp, D.H. & Bareford, K. (2003). *Case Study Analysis of Cuyahoga Valley National Park*. National Park Service: Washington D.C.

Knapp, D.H. & Aycock, J. (2003). *Case Study Analysis of Great Smoky Mountains National Park*. National Park Service: Washington D.C.

Index